Be You Bravely

How to Overcome Life's Struggles by Walking in Faith

Amanda Showell

Trilogy Christian Publishers
A Wholly Owned Subsidiary of Trinity Broadcasting Network
2442 Michelle Drive
Tustin, CA 92780

For information, address Trilogy Christian Publishing

Rights Department, 2442 Michelle Drive, Tustin, Ca 92780.

For information about special discounts for bulk purchases, please contact Trilogy Christian Publishing.

Manufactured in the United States of America

10 9 8 7 6 5 4 3 2 1

Library of Congress Cataloging-in-Publication Data is available.
ISBN 978-1-63769-208-0
ISBN 978-1-63769-209-7 (ebook)

DEDICATION

This book is dedicated first and foremost to our Lord and Savior, Jesus Christ. It is through you I have found my way. You gave me the courage to write this book. You have closed doors that needed to be slammed shut and opened ones to let me see the beauty that was on the other side. Thanks be to you, Lord, for every moment of my life. Thank you for loving me completely, accepting me totally, forgiving me for all my sins, and teaching me how extremely valuable I am.

To my mother, Sandra Showell, I do not even know where to begin. You have stood by me, supported me, and guided me on this journey of life. We are true kindred spirits. Your heartache and struggles were the catalyst for writing this book. Your strength and perseverance in life are the ink on this paper. I could have never asked for a more wonderful mother. What a gift I received the day the Lord blessed me with you as my mom.

To my dearest Kevin, my only true regret in life is that I had to wait so long to find you. God truly blessed the broken road that led me to you. You were the answer to so many, many prayers. You are my joy and my heart. You are my support and strength, my laughter and my smile. I love you with every inch of my being. You have helped me grow into the woman I am, and I know we will be beside each other walking hand in hand for the rest of our lives with Jesus guiding our footsteps.

CONTENTS

PREFACE

As I write these pages, my life is fuller than I could have ever imagined—full of joy, love and happiness, hard work and success, heartache and grief, struggle and strife. I have had two successful careers and a loving family. I have literally danced my way through life and lived it to the fullest extent.

I have also known grief to the greatest depths—the loss of my father when I was 17, two failed marriages, and walking away from a career I had dreamed of since I was a little girl. I have survived a physically, emotionally, and mentally abusive relationship. I know what it is like to have your heart broken by the ones who are the closest to you and your trust betrayed by those you counted on. I know what it is like to think you are not good enough and wonder if you will ever be able make it through to the other side of the storm.

Through all these experiences, this book was birthed. Deep within my soul, I always knew all the struggles, the battles, and the heartaches I have survived would come to be penned on paper to help others who, like me, are just normal, everyday women. I am not a pastor, a psychologist, or a doctor. I do not even have a college degree. What do I have? I have a life that has been filled with many ups and downs—like so many others have faced. It is a life that almost broke me but in turn helped me find my wings. It is a life that has been changed because of my relationship with the Lord. I am you, and you are me. You, the reader, are who inspired me to share my life in the hopes it will encourage you to find your own wings and fly.

Recently, I heard a pastor say, "Don't hide your story. God gave it to you so you could share it with others so they can see the miracles that God has worked in your life." When I heard this, I knew why it was so important for me to write this book and why God has laid on my heart many times to "write your book." God gave me my story and has seen me through my many battles. Life has taught me how the enemy is always waiting to unearth our weaknesses and self-doubts, but our God defeated the enemy long ago, and in Him we find victory. I know that if I can survive what I have endured, then you can survive what comes your way too. I know that the trials we survive here on earth are nothing compared to the glory that awaits us in the kingdom of our Father. I know that it is not always easy to have faith. Most of all, I know my life is not much different than yours. I am a simple woman who has had the chance to do some extraordinary things. I am one of God's children, and I have been blessed in all ways—in the good times and the bad. The Lord is my Good Shepherd.

—Amanda Showell

INTRODUCTION

I am the good shepherd; I know my own sheep, and they know me, just as my Father knows me and I know the Father. So I sacrifice my life for the sheep.

—John 10:14–15 (NLT)

In a sea full of self-help and motivational and inspirational books, why is this one any different? Why choose to read this book over the hundreds of others that are out there? If you have picked up this book to read its pages, I believe God guided you to it, just as much as He has guided me to write it. My greatest hope for this book is that through my journey in life I can make your journey a bit easier. The chapters of this book are written to help you with some of the most difficult aspects of your life and your faith. The topic of each of these chapters could be a book on its own. My desire was to write something that would challenge you to look at many of life's difficulties and how God is with you through them all.

Through this book you will learn that if you accept Jesus Christ as your Savior and open up your life to God, He can ease your hurts, help you through your battles, and give you peace in a world that is filled with turmoil and angst. Jesus is our Good Shepherd, and He knows every sheep in His flock.

Just as a shepherd watches over his flock day and night, guiding them, protecting them, and providing for them, Jesus does the same for us.

My wish is that through these pages you will learn how, with the Lord, you can overcome your past and the fear and anxiety that have come along with it. You will learn to forgive others and yourself, and you will be able to look ahead to the amazing future the Lord has promised each of His children. You will come to know Jesus as your own personal Good Shepherd and grow in understanding that just like a shepherd leads his sheep, God will lead you down the right path if you trust him. When you close the pages of this book, I hope you realize that the person you have been wanting to become has been inside you all along, waiting to be born anew, and that with Jesus by your side, you will be able to walk through your life and *be you bravely* every day.

CHAPTER 1

Why Me? Why Now?

The steps of a man are established by the Lord, when he delights in His way.

—Psalm: 37:23 (ESV)

Have you ever raised your hands in the air and simply asked, "Why me? Why now?" Are you struggling to understand why you have had so many heartbreaks and hurts, so many battles and losses? Do you find yourself asking when life will ever give you a break? You are not alone. Many people have asked those same questions and wondered, "Will life ever not be a struggle?" I know I have asked that many, many times.

The year was 2013, and I was thirty-four years old. I was married, had a home, had a good career, actively volunteered, and was what seemed settled in my life. I had spent the past seventeen years teaching ballroom dancing, my career. It was not always the most profitable or stable profession, so many of those years I worked multiple part-time jobs to make ends meet. Ballroom dancing had been my life since I was nine years old. I had lived and breathed it every day. I had competed with great success. By 2013, I owned my own dance business, had multiple instructors working as subcontractors for me, and was teaching 30 hours of dance lessons a week. My business was booming, and on the outside, my life seemed great, but on the inside, something was missing. I felt empty and lost, without a purpose.

I did not have a close relationship with God at that time in my life. Yet I would still pray and ask Him to bring change to my life. One night on my commute home, I received a phone call that would be an answer to my prayers and the catalyst for a huge change in my life.

I have always loved animals, especially dogs. My heart has always felt at home when I was surrounded by the love of a dog. At that time, my passion for dogs had led me to become incredibly involved in animal welfare. My life outside of work was enveloped by my drive to help and save needy pets. I became a member of the board of a local humane society. I studied dog behavior. I networked on social media for dogs that needed to be rescued. I transported dogs to their new homes and worked with animal rescues to save the lives of as many dogs as possible. I worked hard and fought to see desperately needed change come to local animal shelters.

That fateful night when my phone rang, I was offered a job out of the clear, blue sky. I was asked to take over as the executive director of the local humane society I volunteered for and served on the board. Taking this job was a jewel in my crown of accomplishments and the start of a new chapter in my life. I believed it was an answer to prayer to remove me from the unhappiness and emptiness I felt in my current work.

This "jewel" was a diamond in the rough, to say the least. The shelter had a high kill rate, only enough money in the bank to keep it open for three months, and a less-than-stellar reputation. To make matters worse, the relationship between the county government and the shelter was arduous. Meanwhile, I was running a successful dance business and teaching dance, a mostly stress-free job. I might have not been happy or fulfilled by my career, but life was not a terrible struggle. Now I was walking away from the career I had spent seventeen years building and diving head first into not just a new job but a new life. I called my mother and asked her, "Am I crazy to do this, to give up my business for this mess?" She responded, "Amanda, you have to do what is your purpose, your passion, and what you think God wants you to do." I followed her advice and accepted the job.

I could write an entire book about what my life was like running an open admissions animal control shelter for the next four years. It was a shelter where no animal from the county was ever turned away. I lived and breathed raising money to keep the doors open. On my days and evenings off, I spent hours posting pets on social media and doing whatever it took to get the animals out the door and into a home, no matter how much stress it caused. I brought new programs and new thoughts to the shelter and mended the broken relationship between the county and the shelter.

We (animal control) prosecuted more than seventy-five cases of animal cruelty in four years with a 100 percent conviction rate. I was cursed at, chased after, and physically threatened by the terrible individuals who had committed these crimes. Nothing deterred me from what I was there to do—save animals. I was fearless and passionate.

Through all this, I was still carrying the same longing and emptiness I had felt while running my dance business. I thought my new career would fulfill that emptiness inside of me, but it did not. No matter how much I pushed forward or how hard I worked, I knew something was desperately missing in my life.

My greatest accomplishment at the shelter was my "save rate"—the number of animals reclaimed by their owners, adopted, or sent to another rescue. To put it in layman's terms, it was the number of animals that left the shelter alive. When I started volunteering at the shelter, nearly 50 percent of the animals who came through the doors never left. It was a sad, sad statistic. During my tenure, that number changed. Yearly, 94 percent of dogs and more than 80 percent of cats left the shelter alive. For an open admission shelter (a facility that never turns away an animal no matter how great the need) with an intake rate of more than 1,800 animals in a rural county with just 33,000 people, that was an astounding success. It was something I was proud of. I knew I was doing my job well, but I could never find contentment. No matter how successful I appeared on the outside, I was riddled with sadness, anxiety, and stress on the inside. I was lost.

During the first year of my job as executive director, my second husband left me (more on that later). His leaving was just one more thing that would push me farther into the abyss of self-doubt that I was fighting every day. My work and the shelter were in many ways my sanctuary from our breakup. I worked every day with animals that were unwanted, lost, and in need of rescue—in need of a savior. I could relate to the pain and hurt that many of these pets had suffered. What I had failed to realize was that I needed to be rescued—I needed a savior just as much as they did.

As I continued to battle hurt, loss, and self-defeating behavior, I did what I had always done in hard times. I worked harder and harder with longer hours, more tasks, and added duties. I was trying to fill the emptiness inside of me with work. I believed that if I could just achieve more, raise more money, and save more lives, I would finally find happiness and peace. I was looking for happiness through accomplishments and the approval of others. Yet no matter how hard I worked, it was never enough for the board who ran the shelter. It was never enough for the staff. In some ways, it was never even enough for the animals since there was always more that came through the door needing help and love. Most of all, it was never enough for me. Day in and day out, I went home and cried. I felt like my soul was crushed. I could not believe that this was all my life was meant to be, working day in and day out like a machine.

Many nights through my tears I asked God, "Why me? Why now?" I did not understand why I carried what seemed like the weight of the world on my shoulders and why I could never break free of the burdens that were laid on me. I felt God was silent. I wondered if I had done so much wrong in my life that this was God's punishment. It was not His punishment since God does not punish us (we will discuss this more in Chapter 2). What I failed to understand was that God was standing right beside me, and what seemed like silence was God waiting—waiting on me. He was waiting on me to surrender, waiting on me to come to Him humbly, waiting on me to understand who was ultimately in control.

> Always be full of joy in the Lord. I say it again—rejoice! Let everyone see that you are considerate in all you do. Remember, the Lord is coming soon.
>
> Don't worry about anything; instead, pray about everything. Tell God what you need, and thank him for all he has done. Then you will experience God's peace, which exceeds anything we can understand. His peace will guard your hearts and minds as you live in Christ Jesus.
>
> And now, dear brothers and sisters, one final thing. Fix your thoughts on what is true, and honorable, and right, and pure, and lovely, and admirable. Think about things that are excellent and worthy of praise. Keep putting into practice all you learned and received from me—everything you heard from me and saw me doing. Then the God of peace will be with you.
>
> Philippians 4:4–9 (NLT)

My mom had always talked about the pastors she watched on TV and how powerful their sermons were. Her favorites were Ron Carpenter and Bishop T. D. Jakes. Often when she told me about the word she received from them, it went in one ear and out the other. I was too wrapped up in my life and my work at the shelter. The sermons she watched were the last thing on my mind. But after hearing my mother speak about these sermons over and over, I thought maybe I would take a look. What could it hurt? What I did not realize was that looking would change my life.

One Sunday in early January 2015, I opened my laptop to watch a sermon by Ron Carpenter. Never in my wildest dreams did I realize how much my life would change that day. Even though I had always been a Christian and had known that Jesus was my Savior, I never really knew Jesus. That Sunday was the day I was truly saved. I was born again. I verbally asked Jesus Christ to be my Savior and thanked Him for dying on the cross for me so I could be forgiven of my sins. That day I opened my heart to the Lord and finally understood that in all my sadness and loneliness, I had never been alone. What I would soon come to realize was that the hole inside of me that I had been trying to fill in so many other ways needed to be filled with light—the light that comes from knowing Jesus as my one true Savior.

Little by little after that Sunday, I started to see a change in my life. I am not saying that all of a sudden the heavens opened, my life changed, and I was blessed by miracle after miracle. It was quite the opposite. My struggle and level of unhappiness at my work became greater and greater. I was overwhelmed and in a constant state of exhaustion. The choices I had to make daily at work had taken their toll on me. The constant backstabbing by employees and "friends" left me untrusting and defensive. The pressure of not just running an organization but raising enough money to keep the doors open, the employees with jobs, and the animals alive was an insurmountable mountain I could never finish climbing. I was miserable.

However, I was learning to turn to the Word and to God. I read the words and promises of Psalm 37:32 and knew that my steps were determined by the Lord and I needed to trust Him. Trusting was not my strong suit, so many times, I still repeated those words—"Why me? Why now?" But one time when I asked those questions, the response was different. No longer was there silence. Now a voice deep inside of me said, "It won't be like this forever." Somehow, I knew that voice was telling me the truth, and my trust in the Lord began to grow. I began to trust that the Lord would bring me something new in my life. I just had to learn that He would bring me what He knew I needed in my life in His perfect timing, not mine.

My plan and thoughts were that God was probably going to bring a new career into my life. But my plans and God's were not the same. What I began to understand was that God's plans were much greater than mine. In May 2015, God placed a wonderful man in my life. He was a good man who, like me, had been through so much. He quickly became my best friend and the shoulder I so desperately needed to lean on. While my professional life was falling apart all around me, my personal life was slowly changing. I started to let my guard down and heal from the brokenness inside me. I was not looking for a relationship at the time, but God knew what I needed as He always does. He placed this new man in my life at the right time, not too soon and not too late. God was answering my questions "Why me? Why now?" just not in the way I had expected. God was teaching me that His way and His timing are always perfect, just as He is.

When we ask "Why me? Why now?" we must look to God's promises to understand why certain things happen in our lives. God does not promise us an easy life here on earth. This is not heaven. Jesus, God's own Son, had to suffer and go through trials and temptations while He was here on earth. We cannot expect any different in our own lives. There will be difficulties and hard times. What we must hold on to is the amazing promise that God will always be with us—always. He will always love us, and if we accept Jesus as our Savior, our sins will be completely forgiven. The Apostle Paul wrote in Romans, "And we know that God causes everything to work together for the good of those who love God and are called according to his purpose for them" (Romans 8:28, NLT).

Notice that it does not say everything is good; it says He causes everything to work together *for* good. So no matter what happens in my life, what bad choices I make or what sins I have committed, God will take all those things and work them together for the good of those who love God and are called according to His purpose. This verse is an amazing promise and one of the most well known and most quoted verses in the Bible. Notice that this promise is not for everyone. It is for those who have accepted God's Son Jesus Christ as their personal Savior (those who love God and are called according to His purpose).

God loves everyone, and God wants everyone to be saved. But that only comes through accepting that Jesus died on the cross for your sins. Once you have accepted Jesus as your Savior, you are promised salvation. God wants everyone of His flock to accept His Son, but He gives us the choice. He gives us free will. He will not force us to love Him. Loving Him is our choice, but God loves us all no matter what. That is His promise. Choosing to accept Jesus and know and love God is what I had been missing in my life for a very long time. I had looked to the outside world for fulfillment that could only come from our Lord. Now I was putting my trust in His promise to work all things out for good and moving forward.

I continued as executive director of the animal shelter until fall 2017. Things at the shelter progressively got worse, and finally the immense stress began to physically take its toll on me. In September 2017, I was forced out of my job on medical leave due to ongoing chest pains. For months I had kept it a secret that I was having chest pains and dizzy spells. As the stress increased with the job, the spells increased. Days before, I was supposed to be pepper sprayed and tased as part of new training implemented by my new county supervisor. I had almost blacked out standing in the produce department of the local grocery store.

Frightened by my near blackout, I went to see my physician who immediately scheduled me for an emergency appointment with the cardiologist. My physician gave me a note that I was to be put on light duty and the pepper spray and taser testing would have to wait pending my electrocardiogram (EKG) and echocardiogram test results. My supervisor was infuriated and proclaimed, "There is no light duty in this county." She forced me out immediately on full-time medical leave. I was facing an unknown future with both my health and my career.

While my faith had grown immensely, I could not understand why God was letting all this happen to me. Even with the immense stress and pressure, I still loved my job. I loved working with the animals. Had I been wrong when I thought this career was my calling, my purpose? I was confused and distressed. But now, instead of pushing into my work as my response to stress, I pushed into God. I knew I had to trust His plans for me. "But as for me, I trust in You, O Lord; I say, 'You are my God.' My times are in Your hand: Deliver me from the hand of my enemies and from those who persecute me" (Psalm 31:14–15, NASB 1995).

This has become a Bible verse I pray often. I believe the psalmist was trying to tell us this:

> I trust you, God. I give you everything—my calendar, my schedule, my agenda. I cannot do it without you, Lord. Show me what is important, and help me to not worry about the rest. You are my God. You will protect me. You are my strong fortress. You will shut the door that needs to be closed. In turn, God, You will open a door to the next large blessing You have in store for me.

I saw the cardiologist, who ran a battery of tests on me. The day I walked out of the cardiologist's office, a peace fell over me like I had never felt before. I realized that God was closing the door on my career at the animal shelter and that whatever happened, everything would be okay. For the first time in my life, I understood what it meant to have the peace of God, a peace that lets you remain calm and steadfast even in the worst of storms. A week later, I received a clean bill of health and tendered my immediate resignation from the animal shelter. I moved from one season of life to my next. It may not have been my plan originally, but it certainly was God's. As always, His plans are so much greater than mine.

In this immense time of trial and tribulation, I received the greatest gift—the gift of knowing God and Jesus as my Savior. While I was asking "Why me? Why now?" God was showing me that many times we must walk in the dark before we find the light. If you are walking through a dark time and feel lost and defeated as I did, do not fear. God is with you. He is with you in the storm you are facing. Maybe He is just waiting on you, waiting for you to love Him, learn about Him, and realize the greatest relationship you will ever have is the one you build with our Savior, Jesus Christ.

CHAPTER 2

Would You Get in the Boat?

Immediately Jesus made the disciples get into the boat and go on ahead of him to the other side, while he dismissed the crowd. After he had dismissed them, he went up on a mountainside by himself to pray. Later that night, he was there alone, and the boat was already a considerable distance from land, buffeted by the waves because the wind was against it.

Shortly before dawn Jesus went out to them, walking on the lake. When the disciples saw him walking on the lake, they were terrified. "It's a ghost," they said, and cried out in fear.

But Jesus immediately said to them: "Take courage! It is I. Don't be afraid."

"Lord, if it's you," Peter replied, "tell me to come to you on the water."

"Come," he said.

Then Peter got down out of the boat, walked on the water and came toward Jesus. But when he saw the wind, he was afraid and, beginning to sink, cried out, "Lord, save me!"

Immediately Jesus reached out his hand and caught him. "You of little faith," he said, "why did you doubt?"

And when they climbed into the boat, the wind died down. Then those who were in the boat worshiped him, saying, "Truly you are the Son of God."

When they had crossed over, they landed at Gennesaret. And when the men of that place recognized Jesus, they sent word to all the surrounding country. People brought all their sick to him and begged him to let the sick just touch the edge of his cloak, and all who touched it were healed.

Matthew 14:22–36 (NIV)

If you knew what storm lay ahead of you, would you get in the boat? This question was asked in a Bible study I was attending not long ago. It hit me in a profound way. If you knew what the storm ahead of you was, with all the hurt, trials, and tribulations, would you still make the choice to get in the boat and head into it full on, or would you run the other way? Do you think the disciples would have made that choice to get in the boat if they knew what the storm was going to be like? If your immediate response is "No way! They would have never got in that boat," I would like to challenge you to think differently as we go through these fourteen verses in this chapter. These verses have given me great insight on how we go through the storms we have in our lives. I want you to think about this: If the disciples had known what the storm was going to be like, would they have avoided the storm or gone through it so they could witness the miracle that came because of it?

By human nature, most people would naturally choose not to go through the storms they have had or are currently having in their lives. Most people would choose to go on with their life, happy and content, and stay out of the storm. Just ponder this for a moment: If the disciples had not gotten in that boat that fateful afternoon, they would have never witnessed one of the most amazing miracles in the entire Bible—Jesus walking across the water. Going through the storm brought them an incredible blessing on the other side. What miracle or blessing could God be waiting to show you but has not because you are afraid to go through a certain storm in your life?

Notice in the verses that Jesus made the disciples immediately get into the boat (this was following the miracle of the feeding of the 5,000). It was afternoon when they got in the boat, but it was not until dawn that Jesus came walking across the water to save them. Jesus did not save them immediately. It had been a long night for the disciples who had fought the waves of a rough sea before Jesus ever appeared. I can only imagine the fear the disciples had as they wondered if this storm would kill them. Do you often feel that way, that you are just fighting an ongoing storm? Do you feel it has been a long, dark night and you are praying and praying, but an answer still has not come? I know I have, many, many times. Some storms lasted hours, some days, some weeks, some months, and even some have lasted years. Why does God allow us to go through these storms? Why doesn't He stop them immediately? Is God punishing us?

Contrary to popular belief in our culture, God does not punish us for our sins. Ephesians 1:7–8 (NLT) states, "He is so rich in kindness and grace that he purchased our freedom with the blood of his Son and forgave our sins. He has showered his kindness on us, along with all wisdom and understanding." The ransom for our sins has already been paid. We have been bought for a price. That price was the life of Jesus Christ. He died on the cross so all our sins could be forgiven. He took every sin on Him from all mankind so we could live a life with no condemnation.

Once we accept Jesus as our Savior, we are forgiven of *all* our sins. God does not punish us. But God did give us *all* free will—free will to make whatever choice we want to in life, good or bad. Many storms that happen in our life come from our own doing. Many happen from no fault of our own. With every storm that comes in our life, God is using it not to punish us but to test us, to test our faith and to build our character. We must remember God's promise that He works everything together for the good (Romans 8:28).

In the same Bible study, the pastor who was leading the study made a profound statement: "God doesn't change the storm; God changes the man." Let that sink in. God is changing you in the storm. Perhaps enduring the storm is the only way you will change, and that is why God is allowing the storm to rage in your life. Look back at your life. Think about the storms you have gone through. Think about the person you became after that storm. How much stronger are you because of what you endured? Did you become kinder, more patient, more humble, or more resilient because of that storm? No matter how bad the storm was, in hindsight did it make you a better person? I know my answer is yes. Out of every storm I grew and changed for the better. God used each storm in my life to develop me into who I am today. I am betting that He has done the same for you.

Let's continue to look at Matthew 14:22–36. Peter asks Jesus to prove who He is by asking Him to have him walk across the water. Jesus simply said, "Yes, come." Peter climbed out of the boat and began to walk across the water toward

Jesus. No matter how the waves crashed or the winds blew, if Peter stayed focused on Jesus, he walked through the storm across the water toward Jesus. As soon as Peter took his eyes off Jesus, he became afraid. How many times in life have you been like Peter during a storm? Instead of keeping your eyes on Jesus, you become full of worry, fear, and anxiety. I know I have. So many of us battle anxiety and worry daily. If during the storms of life we could just remember that Jesus told us to come to Him and keep our eyes focused on Him, how much easier it would be to endure the trials in our lives.

As Peter began to sink, he yelled, "Save me, Lord!" Jesus reached out his hand immediately and grabbed him. For me, that is the most beautiful part of these verses. How incredible to know that if we take our eyes off Jesus and start to sink, all we have to do is simply yell, "Save me!" and He will be there with His mighty hand to pull us out of the waters.

Near the end of these verses we see Jesus saying, "You of little faith, why did you doubt?" Some might take that as a criticism of Peter, but I do not. I believe Jesus is showing us here that even if we only have a little faith, faith as small as a mustard seed (Matthew 17:20), and even when we doubt, we only need to call on Jesus. God understands us. He created us. He knows we will have doubts. He understands that our faith will be shaken and small at times. That does not matter to Him. We just need to call on Him, and He will save us from the storm. No matter what type of boat we are in, God is there at the stern to guide us through the storm.

Remember that question, "Would you get in the boat?" Would your answer be different now? We are all going to endure storms in this life. This is not heaven, and life here is not perfect. Jesus suffered and endured great trials. We must remember that the faith we have in Jesus is enough to weather every storm. We must keep our eyes focused on Jesus and understand that God uses storms to teach us about Himself and ourselves. When we come through the storm, we will be a changed person. We will have learned that we must let God take charge of our lives in order to fully surrender to Him. We will see the glory of our Father in a new way.

Do not be afraid of getting in the boat anymore. Do not fear the storm. As Franklin D. Roosevelt said in his inauguration speech of 1933, "We have nothing to fear but fear itself." We must remember, "For God has not given us a spirit of fear, but of power and of love and of a sound mind" (2 Timothy 1:7, NKJV). We must know that no matter how great the storm, Jesus is always with us. His outstretched hand is waiting to pull you out of the water and show you the incredible blessings that lie ahead when dawn breaks and the storm comes to an end.

CHAPTER 3

The Battles That Make You Who You Are

When I had lost all hope, I turned my thoughts once more to the Lord.

Jonah 2:7 (TLB)

When I was seventeen, one of the most pivotal events in my life occurred. I had no idea until many years later just how much this event would affect my life in every way. I did not understand how I would let this event shape me, and sadly, because I did not have the Lord in my life at the time, there were bad choices it would ultimately cause me to make. If I had known the storms that would lie ahead of me at the young age of seventeen (many self-created), I am not sure I would have had the wisdom or courage to get in the boat, the boat we looked at in Chapter 2. Now, because of the grace of God and my relationship with Him, I understand that through Jesus I can live a life with no condemnation or regrets. I understand that the battles we all face help us build the character and wisdom God wants us to have. Now, many years later, I am thankful I got in the boat, not because of the hurts I endured but because of the amazing life that was created after I survived them.

My father was a successful businessman when I was growing up. He owned a car dealership and then became a co-owner in others. He was smart and understood what made a good business. He was as equally kind as he was smart. He believed you always treated the employee and the customer with kindness. He was humble. He was a good man and an amazing father. My brother and I did not want for anything growing up. He was the type of father who was involved in every aspect of our lives. He made every effort to be home at 6:00 each evening so he would have time with his family. In the warm months with long days, our family played baseball and other games after dinner in the front yard of our home in a very small, rural town. My mom, who owned a successful antiques business, often had antique shows on weekends. Dad helped Mom set up the show, took us somewhere fun for the weekend, and got back by Sunday afternoon to help Mom break down the show (a physically grueling task of lifting furniture and boxes of glassware and china). He gave his all for us. He loved his family.

Unfortunately, some people took advantage of my father's kindness. He let a business partner gain his trust, and this partner took advantage of him. After a long battle, my father was forced out of the business he had worked so hard to build. At 54 years old, he was trying to figure out how to start over with a new career. He had broken my mother's trust, and things were rocky between them. Our once perfect life and family had been destroyed by the greed of someone who did not care who he had to step on to work his way to the top. My father and our family were just collateral damage. During this time, I saw the immense stress on my father. He was heartbroken, he was disappointed, and he was lost. While he tried to be happy on the outside, he was broken. He had lost himself and did not know how to find his way back.

By late 1995, my parents had separated, and Dad moved into his own apartment. I was at home by myself the morning of March 14, 1996, when I heard a knock on the door. When I opened the door, my aunt (my mother's sister) was standing in front of me. She said, "Amanda, I don't know how to tell you this, but your father is gone. He died of a heart attack in his sleep, and your brother is the one who found him." In that moment, my whole world shattered, and I stepped into my first storm, one of many to follow. That day I began to fight battle after battle that would last for the next 15 years. I often wondered during those years how my life had become so upside down. Why had life dealt me such an unfair hand? How was I going to get through life without my dad? When my father passed, I became a lost person, and I would struggle for years to find my way back.

Is it not amazing how one moment can be "normal" and the next second our world turns upside down and we enter a storm with 100-foot waves pounding over our boat every ten seconds? That is exactly how I felt the morning my aunt told me my father had passed. Waves of grief, loss, hurt, and disappointment crashed over me all at once. Our family had been through so much with the loss my father's business, and now with his sudden death, a storm of monumental size had overtaken all of us. I simply could not understand why my family had to endure such loss and suffering. I could not comprehend it while I watched others prosper and our world fall apart.

I am sure you have been in a similar boat sometime in your life. I'm sure you have wondered why life is so unfair. You have most likely had many of the same questions I did. It is when we have these questions that we must turn to the God's Word, which will bring us knowledge and comfort. Romans 8:18 (TLB) says, "Yet what we suffer now is nothing compared to the glory he will give us later." The Apostle Paul is telling us we are not promised a life free of trials and difficulties. What we are promised is an eternal life in heaven where we will never have to endure pain of any kind ever again. While we are here on earth, we are growing into the spiritual person God wants us to be so we have the character God wants us to have in heaven. Our life here is like the opening act of the incredible life we will have in eternity with the Lord. The title of this chapter, "The Battles That Make You Who You Are," means the battles we are fighting make us the person God wants us to be—who He planned us to be when He created us. They are building the character that God wants us to bring with us into eternity. These battles are giving us a great testimony—testimonies of how God brought us through the other side and how we are still standing. These stories will help others through their own battles. Our testimonies will show the incredible miracles God can do, even in the biggest storms.

The days following my father's death were a blur. He had been in generally good health. While he was about 50 pounds overweight, he never smoked or drank and had no pre-existing health conditions. Eleven days before, he had turned 55. His death was a shock. My mother, brother, and I went to the funeral home together to pick out my father's casket. Later we stood in the receiving line while people filed by and then filled the funeral home to standing-room-only capacity. I walked up to my father's open casket and placed an award in it I had won at the US National Dance Sport Championship the prior September. I remember the grief, the hurt, the brokenness, the lack of understanding, and the tears. How I remember the tears! I thought they would never cease. Through the immense pain of my father's death, I ultimately learned (albeit many years later) to be an overcomer by trusting in our mighty comforter, Jesus Christ. I survived the storm of my father's sudden death with a testimony of pain, loss, redemption, and healing, all penned in this book. "Praise be to the God and Father of our Lord Jesus Christ, the Father of compassion and the God of all comfort, who comforts us in all our troubles, so that we can comfort those in any trouble with the comfort we ourselves receive from God" (2 Corinthians 1:3–4, NIV).

Most if not all of you who are reading this book have endured the pain of loss—the loss of a loved one, the loss of a job, the loss of a spouse through divorce, the loss of a friendship. How do we handle these times of heartbreak and brokenness? We when go through these great times of loss, we are meant to press into and not just lean on our heavenly Father. That is what He wants. He wants us to turn our thoughts to Him. He wants us to give up complete control. He wants us to delve into His Word to help heal our souls. He wants us to pray and talk to Him openly without fear. He asks us for our trust and to give everything over to Him. He wants us to grieve. He wants us to scream and cry. He understands our pain. He wants us to press into Him so He can comfort us with His unending compassion and love.

God also wants us to do something that is difficult to do while enduring our pain. He wants us to praise Him. 1 Thessalonians 5:16–18 (ESV) says, "Rejoice always, pray without ceasing, give thanks in all circumstances; for this is the will of God in Christ Jesus for you." Notice that it says give thanks in *all* circumstances. It does not say *for* all circumstances. There are some horrible things in our world such as rape, murder, molestation, and cancer that certainly we are not expected to be thankful for. These things are not of God; they are of evil, so we do not have to be thankful for them. What we are expected to do is praise God no matter what the circumstance in our life might be.

As hard as this may sound, there is a reason. Even in the worst of circumstance, there is always something that is worthy of praise. God wants us to hold on to these blessings no matter how small they might seem and realize that each one of them is proof of God's incredible love. Maybe we praise Him for something as simple as the clean water we drink each day or the roof over our heads. Maybe we praise Him for our ability to see, taste, and hear. No matter how difficult the circumstance, we still must learn to praise Him for the blessings we have. We always have blessings we can thank Him for. Many years after my father's death, I learned to praise God for the kindness of my father's passing. My dad never suffered; he never felt any pain. He shut his eyes to go to sleep and awoke to see God in His almightiness standing before him. What a blessing and a gift God gave him. That gift is worthy of all my praise no matter how great the pain of my father's death.

As we learn to push into God during our pain, we need to understand that every hurt we feel, every tear we shed, God feels with us. God has feelings and emotions just like us, and He grieves with us. How do we know this? God created us in His image. Genesis 1:27 (ESV) states, "So God created man in his own image, in the image of God he created him; male and female he created them." Since we are in the image of God, we have emotions just like God. God feels sadness, joy, hurt, and anger, and so do we because He created us to be like Him. God hurts when we hurt.

One of my favorite verses in the Bible is Psalm 56:8 (NLT), "You keep track of all my sorrows. You have collected all my tears in your bottle. You have recorded each one in your book." What an incredibly beautiful image! Close your eyes, and picture how in heaven our Lord has a bottle of all our tears we have cried. He knows every pain and every hurt and has recorded each one in His book. He loves us and wants what is best for us. God hurts just like a parent who hurts when their child hurts. God wants what is best for each of us and hurts when we hurt. He knows what is best for us, even in the hardest times. Our Father understands hurt and loss unlike we have ever known. God knew what Jesus, His only begotten Son, would endure here on earth, but He sent him here to die for our sins anyway. The hurt and pain God felt when He saw His son tortured, beaten, and crucified is unimaginable. Yet God endured that grief so all His children could be forgiven and live in eternity with Him.

As we take comfort in understanding that God feels each of our hurts and pains, we need to also understand that just as we suffer here on earth, Jesus did as well. He endured every pain and emotion that we must endure. Jesus knew temptation, loss, anger, sorrow, grief, hatred, mockery, and betrayal. He endured humiliation, abuse, horrific torture, and execution in the most excruciating way possible—Roman crucifixion. Jesus suffered even though He had never committed one sin. Jesus was perfect, yet He had to endure more pain than we could ever possibly imagine. Jesus paid the price for our salvation through His suffering and pain. "Christ suffered for our sins once for all time. He never sinned, but he died for sinners to bring you safely home to God. He suffered physical death, but he was raised to life in the Spirit" (1 Peter 3:18, NLT). We should take comfort knowing we are never alone in our pain because Jesus has felt every pain we have felt. We should praise our Father and know that God let Jesus pay the highest price possible for us because He loved us that much. That is certainly worth all our praise and thanksgiving.

The battles that make us who we are will never be easy to fight. They will knock us down and make us doubt ourselves and our faith. As we go through each of these battles in life, we must turn to God and remember that He is our mighty fortress and stands strong with us through each of our storms. As Jonah said when he was in the belly of a whale, "When I had lost all hope, I turned my thoughts once more to the Lord" (Jonah 2:7, TLB). When everything seems lost, turn to Him. He is our light in the darkest times of our lives, helping us overcome and grow into the person He wants us to be. While we march through each one of these battles, we must carry our knowledge of the goodness of God as our sword and our shield, knowing the incredible promises of what awaits us in eternity with our Father.

CHAPTER 4

The Waves Keep Rolling

Fear not, for I have redeemed you; I have called you by name, you are mine. When you pass through the waters, I will be with you; and through the rivers, they shall not overwhelm you; when you walk through fire you shall not be burned, and the flame shall not consume you.

Isaiah 43:1–2 (ESV)

I finished high school at the end of January 1996, a little over a month before my father passed. I had planned to attend my graduation ceremony in June, but graduation or anything to do with high school was the last thing on my mind. I was focused on one thing and one thing only: my future career.

I had been competing in ballroom dancing (also known as DanceSport) since I was ten years old. By the time I was fifteen, I was competing at the highest level offered to amateur dancers, the open division. In my final year of competing as an amateur, I won all but one competition in my specialized category, the international standard ballroom. In November 1995, a week before my seventeenth birthday, I won the Ladies Pro-Am (professional – amateur couple) A Championship at the Ohio Star Ball. If you are not a ballroom dancer, you must be thinking, "Ohio? How important can that be?" Well, the Ohio Star Ball is the biggest ballroom dancing competition in the world with more than seven days of nonstop dancing and more than 11,000 entries. The Ohio Star Ball would go on to become the World Pro Am Championships several years after I won my title. To win in Ohio was a big deal. It was a dream come true. I had worked so hard and sacrificed so much for my career, and at that moment, I was on top of the world. The next step was to graduate from high school and turn professional. As a professional, I would compete against the best in the world and be able to teach dancing to others and earn a living. I was focused and determined to be the best I could be.

The caveat with professional competitive ballroom dancing is that you must have a professional partner to dance with (as an amateur, I could dance with my instructor). After I won the Ohio Star Ball, I began my search for a professional dance partner. I had a couple tryouts with potential dance partners, but for different reasons, they were not the right fit. While I was looking for a partner and starting my career, my father passed. But even in my grief, I pushed forward, determined to find a professional partner.

One fateful afternoon about a month after my father's passing, my teacher called to tell me he had found a partner for me. He was the perfect height and size (particularly important in dancing). I was beyond excited. I would have to travel to New York City to try out with him. For this young, small-town girl with big dreams, a trip to New York City was the icing on the cake.

Amid all this excitement in my life, I failed to realize something especially important—I needed time to grieve. Instead of grieving and taking time to understand the pain and hurt I was going through, I pushed it aside and focused on something that was all-encompassing in my life. I was looking for something to fill a huge void that was now in my life. I was looking to outside sources to bring me happiness. What I did not realize is that you cannot look to others to bring you happiness or contentment. Happiness is a choice, and true contentment can only be found when we put our relationship with God first, not when we idolize something else. I had begun to idolize my career and success. I thought that in finding a partner, starting my career, and becoming successful, I would fill the void left by my dad's death. I was wrong. Instead, I began walking down a long road of disappointment and destruction. I was getting ready to enter the next storm I was going to go through—a storm of my own creation, a storm that would almost take my life.

In about a week, I met the man who would be my professional partner. The day I met him, I thought my dreams were coming true. He was a Russian immigrant who had come to the states the year before. He was an accomplished dancer who had competed extensively overseas. Even though he was ten years my senior, the substantial age difference did not matter to me. All that mattered was the potential I saw for a dynamic dance partnership that could achieve great success. I was blinded by the lust of success and notoriety.

For six weeks, I traveled to New York City to rehearse with my new dance partner, who very quickly also became my personal interest. I had never had a boyfriend, and having an older, more mature man take an interest in me made me feel special and loved. What I failed to realize was that I was replacing what was missing in my life—love from my father—

with what I thought I needed, a boyfriend, a dance partner, a career. I was forcing everything to happen in my life the way I thought it should be. I was as far from God as I could get. My actions were not just creating a simple storm in my life; they were creating a hurricane.

Six months after meeting my dance partner, we were married in a small civil ceremony. He needed a green card in the United States, and getting married was the perfect way for him to secure his future here. We wed in October 1996, a little over a month from my eighteenth birthday. Deep down I knew marrying him was not the right thing, but I was caught in a whirlwind that I simply did not know how to escape from. We would keep our marriage secret for almost a year. In August 1997, we had a beautiful church ceremony like many girls dream of. By then I was already living a nightmare.

For the five and a half years our marriage lasted, I endured verbal, mental, and physical abuse. My husband had a terrible drinking problem, and when he drank, the abuse got worse. He also liked other women and made no effort to hide his numerous extramarital affairs. I was living a life of shame and embarrassment. I tried to hide the abuse and infidelity from of our friends, colleagues, and family. The worse the abuse got in our relationship the farther I pushed everyone away. The humiliation I carried around was a burden I did not want to share with anyone. During that time, my health began to diminish. I had constant stomach problems from the stress I was living under. My body had whittled down to ninety-five pounds on a five-foot-eight-inch frame. I was skin and bones. I was in a battle for my life, going through a storm and holding on to nothing more than a small plank of wood. What I did not understand at the time was that even though I did not have a personal relationship with God, God had a personal relationship with me. "For I hold you by your right hand— I, the Lord your God. And I say to you, 'Don't be afraid. I am here to help you'" (Isaiah 41:13, NLT).

As a child, I knew we were a Christian family and that my parents both believed in Jesus. At one time, both of my parents were active in the local church, but that had ended quite early in my life. I was christened as a child and knew who Jesus was, but I did not have a relationship with Him. I knew Jesus had died for me, but to say that I understood who Jesus was and the role He had and would always play in my life would be a far stretch. I did not understand that I should lean on Him, push into Him, trust Him, and ask for His help in all things. Even though I was not close to Jesus, He was close to me. Jesus would be with me and guide me to safety, calming the waves of the storm and bringing me safely across to the seashore. In this storm, I would slowly start the journey of learning who Jesus was to me and how He had truly saved me.

One night when my husband was on another verbally abusive drinking rampage, I locked myself in the bedroom to escape him as I often did. I cried as I thought about his words—telling me I was stupid, worthless, and would never be anything without him. I had begun to believe these things about myself and could not imagine how I could ever get myself out of this situation. I did not know who to turn to or where to go. At times, the thought of taking my life instead of living through the nightmare I was in seemed to be the easier option. That night as I sat in the bedroom, something inside me kept drawing my attention to the drawer in the nightstand beside the bed. Finally, I reached over and opened the drawer to find something I had placed there long before. It was a small, old, dusty Bible that had belonged to my father when he was a child.

In that moment of sadness, fear, self-doubt, and hopelessness, I was drawn to do something I had never done before. I opened the cover of the musty, little Bible and began reading. The pages were thin and fragile, the words tiny. I did not know where to begin, so I simply flipped through the pages until I stumbled upon the book of Psalms. I was immediately compelled to read the 23rd Psalm.

> The LORD is my shepherd. I shall not want. He makes me lie down in green pastures; He leads me beside quiet waters. He restores my soul; He guides me in the paths of righteousness for the sake of His name. Even though I walk through the valley of the shadow of death, I will fear no evil, for You are with me; Your rod and Your staff, they comfort me. You prepare a table before me in the presence of my enemies. You anoint my head with oil; my cup overflows. Surely goodness and mercy will follow me all the days of my life, and I will dwell in the house of the LORD forever.
>
> Psalm 23 (BSB)

In that moment I felt a warmth within my soul like I cannot explain. As I read those six verses over and over, a peace came over me that was like nothing I had ever experienced. The confusion and self-condemning thoughts in my mind stopped.

I knew in that moment I was not alone and that I could never, ever consider taking my life again. Reading that dusty, old Bible, I began to learn I had a Shepherd and that even in the valley I was in, I no longer needed to fear. I could not begin to comprehend the immense depth of those verses. At that moment, I understood all I needed to—that God was always with me. God had come to me in my darkest hour of need, taken me out of the deep pit of despair, and shined on me His incredible love and light. He showed me who He was, and in one of the darkest moments of my life, amid a great hurricane, battling never-ending tidal waves, I found Him.

God is with us every moment of our lives, but ultimately it is our choice to find Him, seek Him, and build a relationship with Him. It is our choice to either endure the storm alone or let God be the one who leads us through the storms of our life. My storm was a self-created one. But certainly I did not cause or create the abuse I was enduring. What I did cause was the wheel that was set in motion by a rash of hasty choices that led me into a relationship and situation that I should have never put myself into. Recently, I heard Pastor Steven Furtick speak of self-created storms. He said that often the first storm that comes into our lives is out of our control (for example, my father's death), but during that first storm, through bad choices and decisions, we create more storms of our own accord. We can avoid these self-created storms by seeking the guidance and wisdom of our Lord through prayer, worship, and studying the Word. Yet if we create a storm of our own, God will use it to teach us and build our character. He will walk with us through the middle of the storm and bring us to incredible blessings that await us on the other side. This is His promise to us. What an amazing promise that is!

Much of what happened while I was married to my first husband is a blur in my memory. I have an extremely hard time recalling specific events during those five and a half years, and that is fine with me. Events that occur in the past are not meant to be rehashed over and over in our minds. I believe that God sometimes allows us to forget events for a reason. Proverbs 4:25 (NIV) says, "Let your eyes look straight ahead; fix your gaze directly before you."

By forgetting those events, we can move on from the past that is weighing us down into the future He wants us to have. The Apostle Paul wrote in Philippians 3:13 (NLT), "No, dear brothers and sisters, I have not achieved it, but I focus on this one thing: Forgetting the past and looking forward to what lies ahead." Our gaze is to be forward on what God has in store for us, not on what lies behind us. Even though many events of those years are gone from my mind, one series of events stands out clearly. Not long after the night I opened that Bible in my nightstand, some events happened that showed me just how the Lord was planning to lead me out of that storm.

On September 11, 2001, I was three months from turning 23 years old. I was still with my husband, but in my mind, I knew I needed to make a plan that would allow me to leave him, get away from the abuse, and end the career I now held with great disdain. I was in the gym on the elliptical that fateful morning that would change the course of history for the United States. As I exercised, I saw everyone gathering around the TVs at the gym. I suddenly realized something terrible was happening. A plane had hit one of the Twin Towers in New

York City. In a matter of minutes, a second plane flew into the towers, and the words *terrorist attack* came across the bottom of the newsfeed on the TV. I was filled with fear and horror. I returned to our apartment and woke up my husband. We decided that leaving the city would be the safest thing to do, so we packed up our suitcases and left our apartment in Wilmington, Delaware, and drove to my mother's home on the Eastern Shore of Maryland.

The events that unfolded over the following hours and days were horrifying. Seeing the images of people jumping out of the towers, choosing to commit suicide over being burned alive, is an image that is forever etched in my mind. Like all Americans, I shed buckets of tears for all the lives lost, all the suffering, all the tragedy. Deep inside, I was secretly crying for another reason. I was crying for myself. I was crying knowing that nearly 3,000 people woke up that morning thinking they would come home that night to their loved ones and never returned. Their lives were lost in an unthinkable, tragic event. At the same time, I was crying because I was living a lost life and realized in that moment that I had to make a change. I knew I could not keep living the life I was living. I had a precious gift called life, and so many had lost theirs that day. I needed to live my life to the fullest. It was time for me to stand up to the storm I was in. God had promised in Psalm 23 to walk with me and guide me, and I finally had the courage to take Him up on His promise.

Over the next weeks I created a plan to start a new life for myself and walk away from the abuse once and for all. I never spoke a word to anyone about it. The week before Thanksgiving 2001, I stepped off the competition dance floor knowing in my heart that it would be the last competition I would ever compete in. A few weeks later, I waited until my husband was gone and packed up everything I could in my car. I left and never looked back. I moved back home with my mom, and on December 26, 2001, I filed for divorce. Three months later, the divorce was granted. The waves stopped rolling, and I was no longer in my boat trying to battle a ferocious storm. I was standing with the Lord on the seashore, His footprints next to mine. He had saved me. Reading His Word and His promises had saved me. The Lord saved me when I realized I was not alone in my pain and despair but He was with me. It would be many years before I would develop a close relationship with Jesus, but I know God saved my life that year. Through Him I realized that life was supposed to be much more than just enduring. It should be about living—living the life that Christ died for us to have, living with a purpose, a purpose in Christ.

No matter how big the waves are in your storm, no matter how fast they are rolling, there is always hope—hope in the promises of our Lord Jesus Christ. No matter how alone we feel, He is always there. If you are still here walking this earth, know that God is not done with you. He has great plans for you. No matter how great your storm is, even if it is of your own creating, God will work everything out for good. Remember when Moses stood on the shore of the Red Sea trying to save the Israelites from Pharaoh? God did not remove the obstacle, the sea that stood in front of Moses. Instead, He parted the waters and led His people across to safety on the other side (Exodus 14). If you give yourself to Jesus, trust in Him, and push into Him, He will do the same for you.

CHAPTER 5

Letting the Door Close

As Pharaoh approached, the Israelites looked up and saw the Egyptians marching after them, and they were terrified and cried out to the LORD. They said to Moses, "Was it because there are no graves in Egypt that you brought us into the wilderness to die? What have you done to us by bringing us out of Egypt? Did we not say to you in Egypt, 'Leave us alone so that we may serve the Egyptians'? For it would have been better for us to serve the Egyptians than to die in the wilderness."

Exodus 14:10–12 (BSB)

I find these verses so remarkably interesting. The Israelites had been slaves to Pharaoh for more than 400 years. Yet when the fear of the unknown future lay ahead, they criticized Moses and asked why he had brought them out there in the desert. Why didn't he just leave them in Egypt? The Israelites were struggling with God closing a door, even though it was a door of slavery and abuse, because they did not like the uncertainty of what was on the other side. Have you ever struggled like the Israelites? Have you tried to keep a door open that God wants to close because you fear the future? I know I certainly have.

Many times in life one of the hardest things we have to do is let a door close and move on to what lies ahead, which is often an uncertain future. We want to hold on to the past. We want to hold on to what is familiar even if that familiarity is hurtful and brutal. But when we accept Jesus as our Savior, we are born again. "Therefore, if anyone is in Christ, he is a new creation. The old has passed away; behold, the new has come" (2 Corinthians 5:17, ESV).

With Christ, we get a fresh start, a new life with Jesus as our high priest, our Lord, our Savior. Accepting Christ as our Savior is just the start of our new life with Him. As we grow in our relationship with Jesus, we must learn to trust God in all ways and in all things. We must trust Him even when that means change in our life that we are unsure about. God often closes a door in our life because it is the only way He can move us into our new life with Him. Removing unfavorable situations or people is the way He opens the door to new blessings in our lives. It is also another way He develops our character. It is essential that we realize these things and let God take control. We need to stop pulling on the door handle, trying to not let it close out of fear of change. We need to trust the Lord and the good plans He has for us.

The day I loaded my clothes in my car and drove away from Wilmington, I knew I was letting the door close on more than just an abusive marriage. The door was closing on my job, a business I had built, and my competitive dance career. That was one of the scariest days of my life. In terms of the physical world, I had nothing left. My job, my career, and my relationship were gone. I left Wilmington with just $50 to my name. Due to my competitive ballroom dancing career, I had chosen not to go to college after high school, so I realized my job options at the time were limited. I was emotionally drained from years of living in an abusive relationship, and because of the abuse, I had no sense of self-worth. As I watched one door after another close in every area of my life, I sensed a great peace about the choices I was making. This peace came from knowing that while everything seemed like it was falling apart, I knew Jesus was working to put all these broken pieces together to help me start a new life. It was His love and reassurance that gave me the confidence to allow every door around me to shut.

I moved back in with my mom and tried to restart my life back in rural Maryland. My dream was to move to California and continue my dance career, but I did not have the financial resources to make that happen. I am so grateful that I did not have the resources to travel out West because I would have been creating yet another storm in my life. God put me exactly where He wanted me when I moved back home.

Once I left Wilmington, I immediately stopped contact with everyone I knew from that time in my life—my students, my colleagues, my friends, and most importantly, my soon-to-be ex-husband. I knew that distancing myself from everyone was a choice I had to make. It would be the only way for me to move on and start a new life away from all the hurt and abuse I had suffered. I knew that if I were to ever have a chance to move on from the past, I would have to let every door close on that aspect of my life. What I did not understand was that by letting those doors close, I was also letting God begin the healing process that had to occur inside of me. Sadly, that healing process took many years, not because of God but because of me. It would be more than twelve years before I would utterly understand what it was to have a relationship with Jesus as my best friend. Once I learned that my peace was found in Jesus and not others, my life changed.

I hope that by reading this book you will learn these hard life lessons much faster than I did. In life we learn in two ways: from our own personal experiences (usually a much harder, longer, and more painful path) or from the experiences of others. My prayer is that through this book and through my testimony you will be able to move on and out of your storms that trouble your life much faster than I did. I hope you will learn to lean on Jesus and let Him close doors in your life that need to be shut. My desire is that my experience will show you that if you have the Lord in your life, you can endure any hardship, any struggle, any pain. God never wastes a hurt. He will use your situation to help others walk through their own storms. But you must let Him close the doors of your past that are holding you back so you can move forward, so God can use you for His purpose. No matter how frightening it is, you can walk through that door and out of the deepest, darkest depths of hurt, abuse, and suffering and enter the light that God wants you to live in.

Are you now ready to let God close the door on what He needs to and start a new life, trusting and resting in God? Maybe you are like twenty-three-year-old me. You might be starting over from the bottom with what you feel like is nothing. I believe sometimes God needs us to start from the bottom. It is at the bottom where faith grows the strongest. When we have nothing else left, we can still depend on Him and His promises. It is okay to start your life over, no matter what age you are. It is okay if you feel like you are starting your life over from scratch. It does not matter to God. He is here to help us no matter how far we have fallen. He is always here with His hand out to rescue us out of the deepest pits of despair (Psalm 40:2).

When you find yourself at one of these low points in your life, as we all will, there is one thing you can do besides pray. Open the Word of God (the Bible), and let His promises refresh you. By some accounts, God makes more than 7,000 promises to us in the Bible—promises of total forgiveness, complete acceptance, total unconditional love, hope, and prosperity, just to name a few. We must learn to rest in God and understand that He has promised to be with us always, to strengthen us, and to protect us. We can count on those promises because God *never* breaks a promise. Things might not happen on our time schedule or as we think they should, but God always comes through with what is best.

Allowing God to shut a door in your life while not knowing what awaits you on the other side is one of the greatest ways to build your trust and faith in Him. By letting go and giving up control, we start to see God work in our lives in ways we could never possibly imagine. He will begin opening doors and bringing opportunities for us so we can obey and follow His words and believe in His Son, Jesus Christ.

What we must understand is that God will most likely shut many doors throughout our lives. Though it may be difficult, we must realize that it is part of the process we must go through in order to develop more Christ-like characteristics in preparation for our lives in eternity. Leaving an abusive marriage at the age of twenty-three was not the only time I had to let God close doors in my life. He has had to close many more doors, some that I realized at the time and some that I did not. He closed doors on friendships that were not honest, true friends. He closed doors that prevented me from making bad choices. He closed the door on my job as the director of an animal shelter when the stress of it became so great it was literally killing me. He would also close the door on my second marriage.

About a year after my divorce, I met someone who would become my second husband. He was a cook at the hotel where I worked. When we met, he was going through a divorce, so it was easy to relate to each other in many ways. We seemed to have a lot in common, and I quickly fell head over heels. He did not have a place to live, so I rushed ahead of God's plan and let this still married man move into my apartment just three weeks after we met. I thought I needed to help him and rescue him, but I was wrong. Years later I learned that as much as we want to rescue someone, it is only through their own will with the help of God that they can be rescued. While I was busy trying to rescue my second husband, I really needed to be rescuing myself.

His divorce was finalized the year after we met, and we got married in April 2006. My second husband and I would be married for eight years and in a relationship for a total of eleven years. While our relationship had its issues and ups and downs, it seemed like nothing compared to what I had been through in the past. I was not happy in our relationship, but I always hoped things would change. I had become complacent and accepted that a mediocre life was what I was destined for. I had rationalized that since I was not being abused, being simply unhappy was not so bad. In my heart I felt undeserving of a special, wonderful relationship that a marriage should be. I felt this was as good as I could get, so I stayed.

During those eleven years, I repressed my faith and my relationship with God. My husband was an atheist, and I hid the relationship I had with God from him. If I ever brought up God, he ridiculed me and made me feel foolish. To keep the peace, I just kept quiet. Hiding my relationship with God was a huge mistake. I would learn later in life that *nothing* is more important than my relationship with God and I should never be ashamed of Him. If you think you need to hide your love for God to keep peace in a relationship, you should run as fast as you can. Hiding your relationship with God is never God's will. In Luke 9:26 (NIV), Jesus says, "Whoever is ashamed of me and my words, the Son of Man will be ashamed of them when he comes in his glory and in the glory of the Father and of the holy angels." We should never be ashamed of our love for Jesus because Jesus is *never* ashamed of His love for us, no matter what we do, no matter what mistakes we make. Even though we might try to hide our love for Him from the world, He will never hide His love for us.

In May 2014, I went to Daytona Beach, Florida, for a work conference. While I was there, I sensed things were very odd with my husband. When I called him in the evenings, he spoke no more than five minutes before he quickly got off the phone. When I flew home, he refused to come to the airport to pick me up, so I had to wait more than two hours to take a shuttle that would drop me off at a hotel about 20 minutes from where we lived. He picked me up there. His behavior had become increasingly erratic and strange. He had quit his job without telling me so he could attend school full-time, which left me to pay all our bills. Without any words being spoken, I knew he was slowly pushing me away, but I was lost about what to do. What I did not realize was that I did not need to know what to do. God, as always, was in control, and He was getting ready to shut another door in my life that desperately needed to be closed.

The morning after I returned from Daytona Beach, I woke up bright and early and prepared for the long day ahead of me. I worked all day at the animal shelter, came home briefly, and then went to play music for one of the local ballroom dancing clubs until 11:00 p.m. Since my husband had quit his job, I had to work overtime just so we could scrape by. I was easily working eighty hours a week. The pressure of keeping everything going and working a huge number of hours each week was taking a toll on me mentally and physically. Once again, I was stuck in another storm that I was not sure how to get out of. It was another storm of my own creating.

That day when I came home from my first job to change my outfit so I could go to the second job, I got the courage to finally ask my husband what was wrong. He looked at me blankly and simply stated, "I am not happy. I am moving out." That was it. Two days later, he did just that. He left, and our eleven-year relationship was over. I filed for divorce a month later. In the blink of an eye, the door of our life together closed, and I was now a two-time divorcee at the age of 35.

After the initial shock of our separation, it did not take long for me to realize that his leaving was the best thing that could happen to me. I already had the responsibility of all the bills and mortgage, and now I did not have the responsibility of his bills as well. When I came home at night, I no longer dreaded walking into the house. My house was slowly becoming a home that was no longer filled with strife and animosity, just peace and love from my three dogs.

I started to find who I was, but most importantly, the closing of that door was what led me eight months later to be born again, to accept and finally understand what it meant to have Jesus Christ as my Savior, and to begin my daily walk with the Lord. God always has a plan, and His plans are so much better and bigger than we could ever dream. We must focus on what waits ahead of us and not look back or long for what was behind us because it was comfortable and familiar.

> For our present troubles are small and won't last very long. Yet they produce for us a glory that vastly outweighs them and will last forever! So we don't look at the troubles we can see now; rather, we fix our gaze on things that cannot be seen. For the things we see now will soon be gone, but the things we cannot see will last forever.
>
> 2 Corinthians 4:17–19 (NLT)

We are reminded in these verses that the troubles we have here on earth will not last long and that they help produce for us a glory in heaven that will last forever. Every trouble we have in this life, whether we create them ourselves or they are created by outside sources, cannot outweigh the promises or the goodness of God. So stop looking back at the door that is closing behind you. Step forward with God, and move into the light of the promises that our Father gives us. Trust me, you will not regret it!

CHAPTER 6

Finding Strength in Your Struggles

Have I not commanded you? Be strong and courageous.
Do not be frightened, and do not be dismayed, for the Lord
your God is with you wherever you go.

Joshua 1:9 (ESV)

It was February 1979 during a terrible blizzard that was pounding the East Coast of the United States. My parents were with me at Johns Hopkins University Hospital in Baltimore City, Maryland. I was only ten weeks old, and my mother was handing me over to the nurses who were preparing me for surgery to have a kidney removed. I was born with four kidneys, duplicate bilateral kidneys, or simply an extra set of kidneys. One of the extra kidneys in my little body was not functioning properly and needed to be removed. It would be a difficult surgery with a long recovery. The surgery was successful, and when I was returned to my parents, I had one less kidney and a scar over half the width of my tiny body.

My doctors told my parents I would struggle developing certain motor skills due to the surgery and would be slow to learn to walk. But at the age of six, I joined my first ballet class. In second grade, I drew a picture of a dancer and wrote on it that I wanted to be a dancer when I grew up. At the age of nine and a half, I began ballroom dancing, which led me to an extremely successful amateur and professional career. I competed at an elite level and went on to teach dancing as a profession. No one in my family at that time was a dancer. God had given me a talent, a gift for dancing. He had also given me and my family a major struggle, a surgery to overcome and a permanent scar to remind me of that struggle.

As an adult, I started looking at that scar on my side as more than just a scar. It was a reminder of the strength that was birthed in me when something inside of me was not working and needed to be removed. Often our scars are not physically noticeable like mine is, but they are there. They are emotional scars, mental scars, scars from a broken heart; I could go on and on. While each of these scars is created differently, they all come from a place of hurt and pain. A scar of any kind shows we have endured. A scar is a sign of survival, a sign of strength, a sign of courage—a sign that we can overcome.

What needed to be removed from me as a ten-week-old child was physical, but I believe that God often removes people, things, and situations from our lives so we are able to move into the next season of life. The removal of these things and the closing of doors can be hurtful, as we saw in the prior chapter. Through the purging process that happens in our lives, we feel hurt and heartache, and in turn, scars develop. Yet with these scars and the removal of toxic people, situations, and things comes a newfound strength.

When we lean into God during these times and understand that God must change and remove things to help us grow into the person He wants us to become, we are not just developing strength. We are growing our faith. It is through our faith that we can endure the hardest moments of our life. It is at these moments we realize that there is strength in every struggle we have. That strength is God's almighty power that gets us through even the very darkest of times. Just as God told Joshua that He was preparing him to lead the Israelites into the Promised Land after the death of Moses, we are not to be afraid or discouraged because God is with us wherever we go (see Joshua 1:9 at the beginning of the chapter).

> These trials will show that your faith is genuine. It is being tested as fire tests and purifies gold—though your faith is far more precious than mere gold. So when your faith remains strong through many trials, it will bring you much praise and glory and honor on the day when Jesus Christ is revealed to the whole world.
>
> 1 Peter 1:7 (NLT)

As hard as trials and struggles may be, we have such an amazing promise in 1 Peter 1:7. The trials we endure purify our faith the way fire purifies gold. If you have ever seen gold in its natural state, it is not beautiful. It must undergo a refining process that involves fire and close attention by a goldsmith. During this process, all the impurities are removed, producing a pure product. The result is the beautiful, strong metal that has been made into jewelry for centuries.

God is our goldsmith, refining us and removing the impurities in us as we go through the tests and trials of life. God uses these tests and trials to change us and refine us, working us into a pure product just as the goldsmith does. We gain strength from our struggles. God does not always create these trials, but He lets us go through them *because* He loves us so much. He wants us to develop Jesus-like qualities and characteristics, referred to as the fruit of the spirit (Galatians 5:22–23). As we remain strong in our faith through our trials, not only do we grow, but we also honor Jesus and show the world that no matter what our life brings, Jesus Christ is our Savior, and He is with us always. Through our struggles, we show the world our unshakable faith.

I have often wondered how my parents felt (or any parent must feel) when they watched their child go in for a surgery over which they had no control. Overwhelmed, helpless, and frightened are the first words that come to my mind. These are the same words that follow us around as we go through great struggles. Then I think about the moment the surgery is over and successful. Exhaustion, elation, and a sense of relief are the emotions that every parent must feel in that moment. The recovery process for the child begins, but at the same time, it's a recovery process for the parents. It's a mental and emotional recovery. The emotions a parent feels when their child comes out of surgery and the mental recovery process are like what anyone feels after surviving a great trial in their lives. We all must go through recovery. Some of us go through many recoveries—physical, mental, and spiritual. What is important is how we recover and the strength we gain once we are healed. "So we have come to know and to believe the love that God has for us. God is love, and whoever abides in love abides in God, and God abides in him" (1 John 4:16, ESV).

A synonym for the word *abides* is "follow." If we follow in love, then we follow God, and God follows in us. Or insert the word *endure* into that verse; it's also a synonym for the word *abide*. God is love, and whoever endures in love endures in God, and God endures in him. It's amazing how a verse can be transformed by putting in a synonym. I love using the word *endure* in this verse. Sometimes we must endure; that is part of our life here. We endure struggles. But in those struggles, if we endure with love in our heart, if we endure leaning into God, then God endures with us. Once again, we see how Jesus is the strength in our struggles and how He helps us develop the strength of our character that comes from the struggles of our life.

Finding strength in our struggles is not easy. Often we are so busy fighting the storms in our lives that we miss seeing what the storms—the struggles—are trying to teach us. In Chapter 2, I referred to one of the most famous stories in the Bible found in Matthew 14. This is the story of the disciples in a boat during a ferocious storm and Jesus walking across the water and ultimately calming the storm. If you ever attended church or went to Bible school as a child, you are surely familiar with this story. Sometimes the familiarity of the story allows us to miss the great truths that lie within it. I recently heard a pastor speak about how there is one word in Matthew 14:22 that is often overlooked but shows us a deep truth about God and the storms that can happen in our own lives.

"Immediately He made the disciples get into the boat and go ahead of Him to the other side, while He sent the crowds away" (Matthew 14:22, NASB 1995). Did you catch the word? Jesus *made* the disciples get into the boat. Certainly, Jesus knew what was ahead of them. He is God, after all. He knew a storm would come. He knew the apostles would struggle, fear, and wonder if they were going to survive. Jesus also knew He would put out His mighty hand and catch Peter as he started to descend into the water below. Jesus knew He would calm the storm and the winds, and that after everything, He would bring them to the other side.

God always knows. He knows the storms you are going through. He knows the lessons He wants you to learn from each struggle in your life. He knows if you will pass the test of this storm or if you will fail. What God wants us to know is that no matter how hard the struggle is, no matter how great the storm is, we never need to find our own strength. We have always had strength. Strength has been there all along. He has been waiting with an outstretched hand to catch us and bring us to the other side. We do not need to ask God to give us strength. God is our strength, and if we remember to always turn to Him, finding strength in our struggles is not that hard after all.

What struggles are you enduring now or have endured in the past? As we saw in the previous chapters of this book, I have endured many of my own personal struggles—abuse, divorce, betrayal, loss, grief, bitterness. You have endured many of those same struggles. Maybe you are struggling with something else, a struggle with a personal addiction, financial troubles, a mental or physical disability, or an injury. Take a moment and think of a situation from the past and a situation you have come through. Think about what you learned from that situation, how you grew out of it, and the person you became because of that struggle. Think about how you thought you might not make it through but how you came out stronger on the other side. Think about how you found strength in your struggles. Just as you fought through that prior struggle in your life, you can fight through the struggle you are going through now.

What you must remember is that you do not need to go through this struggle alone. Just as the apostles were not alone as the waves from the storm battered their boat, you have an advocate, a protector, a warrior, a solider to help you fight whatever battle you are facing. He has been alongside you all the time. His name is Jesus, and He is a mighty fortress, a strong rock. "Truly he is my rock and my salvation; he is my fortress, I will never be shaken" (Psalm 62:2, NIV). Our rock and our fortress has just been waiting on us to reach out and grasp the hand He has been offering to help us through our battle. Simply speak to Him, pray, and ask Him to be there with you. He will be your partner and your strength through each battle that lies ahead.

God is taking us from glory to glory in this life, from season to season. God does not tell us how we will get from glory to glory, and sometimes there will be seasons of difficulties between seasons of greatness. Each of us will endure those struggles, some small, some monstrous. We will continue to endure struggles until our time here has come to an end and we return home to be with Jesus. What we must learn in our struggles is that we can always find strength during them if we turn to God. He is always with us, and He is always there for us to lean on. Once we have come through a struggle and have leaned on God and His strength, we will find new strength within ourselves. It is often through battles and struggles that we find our true selves, the person God is waiting for us to become.

CHAPTER 7

Learning to Forgive

And whenever you stand praying, forgive, if you have anything against anyone, so that your Father also who is in heaven may forgive you your trespasses.

Mark 11:25 (ESV)

You have survived the storm, you have endured the struggle, and you have fought through your battle with God as your armor, your sword, and your shield. The next step God wants from us is to forgive those who hurt us during the storms in our lives. *Forgiveness* is one of the hardest words in the English language. Someone has hurt you, lied to you, cheated you, or betrayed you. How can you ever consider forgiving them? Why should you forgive them? They are not sorry, so you feel they do not deserve to be forgiven. All these things might very well be true, yet consider that God has forgiven you for every sin and every mistake you have ever made or will ever make. Do you deserve to be forgiven? Maybe not, but that does not matter to God. He forgives us no matter what. His love is unconditional. He loved us so very much that He sent His Son to suffer and die on the cross so we could be forgiven of our sins. "God made him [Jesus] who had no sin to be sin for us, so that in him we might become the righteousness of God" (2 Corinthians 5:21, NIV).

Every one of us has been hurt by someone. That is part of our life here on earth. We get to make the choice to either become bitter or become better. When we carry around anger, hurt, and bitterness, it weighs on us, tires us out, and makes us anxious and unpleasant to be around. What does it do to the person who hurt us? *Nothing!* They are going along with their day-to-day life not spending one moment thinking about you and your hurt. The only person who is harmed when you hold a grudge and do not forgive is you.

For many years I carried around a lot of bitterness and resentment. I was bitter because I saw what had happened to my father and his business. I was bitter because I had endured abuse at the hand of someone who I thought loved me. I was angry because I had been betrayed by people I loved and promises that had been broken. On the outside, I looked perfectly fine. On the inside, I was a mess filled with resentment and hurt. "Be kind to one another, tenderhearted, forgiving one another, as God in Christ forgave you" (Ephesians 4:32, ESV).

In February 2002, I was driving from Philadelphia back to my mother's house on the Eastern Shore of Maryland. I was still going to Philadelphia one day a week to teach after leaving my abusive first husband. Money was short, and going to Philadelphia gave me an extra source of income. Driving two and half hours each way, teaching all day, and seeing my soon-to-be ex-husband (we taught at the same facility) proved to be too much. I had decided that this would be the last day I would make that drive. I said goodbye to all my students and friends, knowing it would be the last time I would see any of them. I was angry and bitter.

As I drove home in rush hour traffic that afternoon, it began raining. Along with the drops of rain from the sky came drops of tears from my eyes. Soon I was sobbing hysterically. My tears were not from sorrow but from anger. I had nothing but pure hate in my heart for my soon-to-be ex-husband. Daily I was reliving in my mind the abuse, the deception, and the cheating he had put me through. It was as if a tape was constantly playing on repeat in my mind. I could not let go of the past and the hurt.

As I mentioned in earlier chapters, my relationship with the Lord at that time was just in the beginning stage. Even though I did not understand much about God, I knew that day in my car that I needed Him more than anything. I literally screamed out as I was driving, "Jesus, take this pain away from me. Take this anger out of my heart. Show me how to forgive and forget." I cried the entire two and half hours home and all through that evening. My soul felt as if it were being torn apart. I asked God to help me forgive my soon-to-be ex-husband for all he had done to me. I asked God to help me move on and to release me from my self-imposed torture of reliving the past. I was on my knees in full surrender to God, knowing that only His mercy could remove me from the turmoil that was destroying me. I believe it is at these moments when we completely surrender ourselves to God, simply having nothing left, that we grow the closest to Him. It is when we give it all to Him that we learn our greatest lessons. My lesson that day was the lesson of forgiveness.

The next morning, I awoke, and God had answered my prayers. A weight had been lifted from my shoulders. I never again felt anger toward my ex-husband. I felt nothing. The memories from that time of my life began to fade until it soon became nearly impossible for me to remember much of what happened during that time. It took time, but I eventually completely forgave my ex-husband for all he had done. I did not forgive him for his sake but for my own sake. I learned to let go of all the hurt that was pent up inside of me, not only from my ex-husband but from all the other hurts I was carrying around. Most importantly, I learned what it meant to forgive and how forgiving someone is a gift to yourself, a gift of freedom, a release from the chains of bitterness that tie us down and steal the joy from our lives.

The day I cried out to Jesus, asking Him to help me learn to let go, He began a process inside of me that would give me the strength to forgive. Throughout the years, I was tested greatly in my ability to forgive. Sometimes the tests were easier than others. Ultimately, I have learned that when I am hurt, I should not seek vengeance but rather forgive the person and move on. I can personally attest that learning these lessons from Jesus has been one of the greatest blessings of my life. "Dear friends, never take revenge. Leave that to the righteous anger of God. For the Scriptures say, 'I will take revenge; I will pay them back,' says the Lord. (Romans 12:19, NLT).

Along with learning to forgive and moving on, it is important to understand God that never wants us to seek vengeance for what was done to us. As hard as it may be, vengeance is not for us to seek, no matter how hurt we have been. Vengeance is for God. Paul reminds us in Romans 12:19 of the promises

God gave to his people. God is a kind, loving, gentle Father, but He is also a just and righteous God. He knows every hurt you have ever felt and who caused that hurt. You are His child, and He promises to protect you. One of my favorite Bible verses is Psalm 91:4 (NLT), "He will cover you with his feathers. He will shelter you with his wings. His faithful promises are your armor and protection." How beautiful is that? God wraps His arms around us and protects us, and His promises in his Word are our armor and our protection. Psalm 91:14–16 (NIV) says, "'Because he loves me,' says the Lord 'I will rescue him; I will protect him, for he acknowledges my name. He will call on me, and I will answer him; I will be with him in trouble, I will deliver him and honor him. With long life I will satisfy him and show him my salvation." God will protect and honor us, and He will seek justice for actions done against us. Our job is to trust God, forgive, and move on.

"God, your God, will restore everything you lost; he'll have compassion on you; he'll come back and pick up the pieces from all the places where you were scattered. No matter how far away you end up, God, your God, will get you out of there" (Deuteronomy 30:3–4, MSG). As hard as it might be once you learn to forgive, you will open yourself up to live the life that Jesus died on the cross for you to have. Jesus not only bought and paid the price for our eternal salvation, He also died so we could have a life filled with joy and peace here on earth. We must take steps to make that happen. One of those first steps is forgiveness—forgiving yourself and others.

One thing I have come to learn recently is that the sooner you forgive someone and move on, the more mature you have grown in your spirituality. Do not feel bad if you are always the first one to forgive. That shows you have gained wisdom and understand what God wants you to do. Forgive, and move on. If you carry unforgiveness in your heart, you are blocking God's blessings. God has promised us many things in His Word, but many of them come with conditions. Having a forgiving heart is one of those conditions. As hard as it might be, now is the time to let go, forgive, and move on from the hurts that are holding you back. Learning to forgive is part of growing in God and becoming who He wants you to be so you can live a life full of joy, hope, and peace, and enjoy the incredible relationship you are meant to have with your Father in heaven.

CHAPTER 8

Accepting the Past and Moving On

If we confess our sins, he is faithful and just to forgive us our sins and to cleanse us from all unrighteousness.
1 John 1:9 (ESV)

Once we learn to forgive others, there is one other person we must learn to forgive: ourselves. Often forgiving ourselves is the hardest thing to do. We so often hold on to the sins of our past and live in the guilt of the mistakes we have made. We allow the dark shadows of our past to linger in our minds. We condemn ourselves and feel we are not allowed to let go of our mistakes and sins. Lack of self-forgiveness is often what holds us back from the greatness of our future that God has promised us.

Along with the anger and bitterness I carried for many years, I also carried an incredible amount of guilt. The burdens of my past mistakes weighed me down like an invisible lead vest I wore everywhere. Long after I had learned to forgive everyone in my life, I still could not forgive myself. I was carrying around the weight of the passing of my father. Even though I consciously knew his passing was not my fault, I carried the weight of the unkind words I had spoken to him at times as a typical teenager. I carried the weight of two failed marriages, ashamed of the poor choices I had made and the failure I thought I had incurred. I carried the weight of the abuse I had endured and the unkind words that had been burned in my mind, causing me to struggle with loving the person I was. I could fill pages with the amount of guilt I had built up inside of me, a lifetime of guilt I was holding on to that I simply could not let go of. "Therefore, there is now no condemnation for those who are in Christ Jesus, because through Christ Jesus the law of the Spirit who gives life has set you free from the law of sin and death" (Romans 8:1–2, NIV).

When I found Jesus, I learned that through Him I was completely loved, valued, accepted, and forgiven. I learned that there is no condemnation or punishment for those who have accepted Christ because when Jesus died on the cross for us, He set us free from all sin and punishment. What an amazing gift we are given! But as with any gift, we must learn to graciously receive it.

Receiving our gift of no condemnation is like receiving a gift from a beloved friend. If my friend gave me a gift, I certainly would not say, "Oh no, I cannot take that. I am not good enough to receive your gift. I am not worthy of the sacrifice you made for this gift or the time, energy, and thought it took to give me this gift! Oh no, I cannot accept this!" Living a life filled with guilt is like turning down one of the gifts Jesus gave us when He died for us. Every time we let ourselves be riddled with guilt after we have accepted Jesus as our Savior, we are telling Him we do not want the gift He died on the cross for. Jesus is our best friend, and He sacrificed everything so we could receive the gift of salvation and be set free from the law of sin and death.

So how do you receive your gift? You must accept it, then believe it, and finally receive it. First, we accept the truth that Jesus is the Son of God and that He died on the cross for our sins and was resurrected on the third day. Second, we must believe these facts are true and ask Jesus to be our Savior (be born again). Finally, we must receive the gifts of God's grace by asking for forgiveness of all our sins from our past and present. It's hard to believe it is that simple, but it is. There is nothing we can do to earn forgiveness. We are forgiven because of God's amazing grace. Colossians 2:13–14 (NLT) states, "You were dead because of your sins and because your sinful nature was not yet cut away. Then God made you alive with Christ, for he forgave all our sins. He canceled the record of the charges against us and took it away by nailing it to the cross." Now you must extend that grace to yourself and learn to forgive yourself.

If God can forgive us, why can we not forgive ourselves? Forgiving ourselves is difficult because we have an enemy who wants to remind us of all the mistakes and sins of our past. Satan is the ultimate liar, and he wants us to stay burdened down with the weight of our past. If Satan can hold us back, then he will be successfully keeping one more of God's children from reaching their full potential. Satan's weapon is our feelings, and he will try to control them in every way he can.

"The thief comes only to steal and kill and destroy; I have come that they may have life, and have it to the full" (John 10:10, NIV). In this verse, Jesus is referring to Satan when he speaks of the thief. Satan, our enemy, would like to do everything he can to destroy each of us. Just as a parent hurts deeply when their own child is hurt, God feels the same about us when we are hurt. Satan knows he cannot defeat God. In fact, he already lost. Jesus's life, death, and resurrection defeated the enemy.

Satan knows that if he can get to God's children, if he can tempt us, belittle us, make us believe negative things about ourselves and drive us to live a life overwhelmed with guilt, then he is hurting God. What is incredible is that we *do not* have to give in to the thoughts and lies the enemy tries to feed us. As Jesus stated in John 10:10, He came so we could have life and live a full life. What an incredible promise our God gave us through His Son, Jesus. We have the choice to ignore the enemy and press forward. We can choose to not look back at the past but to forgive ourselves as God has forgiven us and then move on to the life He has promised us in His Word. How do we do that? "We are made right with God by placing our faith in Jesus Christ. And this is true for everyone who believes, no matter who we are" (Romans 3:22, NLT).

Once you understand that through Jesus Christ you are completely forgiven, you can stop looking at the past and focus on the future as God guides your path. Through our belief and faith in Jesus, we are made right with God. I have heard famous author and speaker Joyce Meyers state many times that for years she said to herself every day, "I am the righteousness of God in Christ Jesus" (see Romans 3:22). Write that phrase on a note card, and stick it on your bathroom mirror, in your car, or on your forehead. Put it somewhere so you can remind yourself over and over that no matter what mistakes you have made in your past or what mistakes you might make in the future, you are the righteousness of God in Christ Jesus. Understand that through Jesus you were made right with God. Nothing can change that, no matter who you are or what you have done. "For God has done what the law, weakened by the flesh, could not do. By sending his own Son in the likeness of sinful flesh and for sin, he condemned sin in the flesh" (Romans 8:3, ESV).

For years after the abuse I endured in my first marriage, I was unable to speak about it. I was ashamed and embarrassed that I had ever let myself be in that situation. I just stuffed it deep down inside of me and went on my way, believing I was moving on with my life. Yes, physically I was. From an outsider's perspective, I certainly was well on my way to a fresh start. I was building a new business, I had a new relationship, and I was starting over in a new place. What I did not realize for many years was that all these outward appearances did not mean anything. Spiritually, I was broken. I continued to make bad choices because I could not let go of the past. I could not forgive myself for what had happened. I could not let go of the fact that I had lost my dreams and hopes at the hands of an abuser. I could not let go of the hurt that was so burned into my heart. I believed the life I was supposed to have as a champion ballroom dancer had been ripped away from me. I hated myself for falling prey to someone who wanted nothing more than to destroy the person I was and all I had achieved. I had convinced myself that I had missed my opportunities in life and that what lay ahead could never be as good as what I had lost.

What changed me and taught me to forgive myself and never look back was the incredible love I received when I found Christ. By studying His Word, watching or listening to sermon after sermon, reading devotional books, and praying a lot, I started to realize that through Jesus loving me, I could learn to love myself. I finally understood there was nothing more to be done about the mistakes I had made because through Jesus's death, the debt of my sins had been paid.

Slowly, the dark cloud that filled my spirit was filled with a light—the light from Christ. I knew He loved me and had forgiven me. I knew that what God had planned for me was so much more than what I could have ever imagined. I opened my eyes to the beauty and the blessings that were in my life in abundance. They had always been abundant, even in my darkest times. I had just been too full of self-contempt to be able to see them. I started thanking God every day, even for the small things in my life and the blessings I took for granted. I became purposeful that when the enemy brought thoughts in my mind, I would repeat 2 Corinthians 10:5 (ESV), "We destroy arguments and every lofty opinion raised against the knowledge of God, and take every thought captive to obey Christ." Finally, I forgave myself because I knew God had forgiven me long ago before I was even created.

The title of this book is *Be You Bravely* because that is what I learned to become by accepting and then letting go of the past. That is what I have grown into by forgiving myself. I became "me bravely" when I realized that God was with me every step I take. I became "me bravely" through God and in God. I knew if David could defeat Goliath with a simple stone because of his faith in God (1 Samuel 17), I could defeat anything that was behind me or ahead of me with my faith. I could be brave in anything because "I can do *all* things through Christ who strengthens me" (emphasis added) (Philippians 4:13, NKJV).

Are you ready to *be you bravely*? You have to let God close the doors that need to be shut. You have survived the storms, and you have learned from them. You have started to forgive others, and now you are ready to forgive yourself, right? Are you ready to let go of those binds that have tied you down for so long from carrying a heavy burden of guilt and self-condemnation? If you are, then take that amazing first step, and accept Jesus as your Savior. Open the door, and walk into eternity with your Father. If you have already accepted Jesus as your Savior, then start living the life He died for you to have. Read the Word, go to church, listen to worship music, join a small group or Bible study, pray, and talk to God. Let go of your past, take His hand, and let Him guide you through the future that lies ahead of you. Forgive yourself as He has forgiven you. Resist the enemy, and stop looking back at what is behind you. Focus on today and the joy that each day living with Jesus brings. Be you bravely as you have never been before.

CHAPTER 9

Your Will, Your Way, My Faith

Then Jesus went with his disciples to a place called Gethsemane, and he said to them, "Sit here while I go over there and pray." He took Peter and the two sons of Zebedee along with him, and he began to be sorrowful and troubled. Then he said to them, "My soul is overwhelmed with sorrow to the point of death. Stay here and keep watch with me." Going a little farther, he fell with his face to the ground and prayed, "My Father, if it is possible, may this cup be taken from me. Yet not as I will, but as you will." Then he returned to his disciples and found them sleeping. "Couldn't you men keep watch with me for one hour?" he asked Peter. "Watch and pray so that you will not fall into temptation. The spirit is willing, but the flesh is weak." He went away a second time and prayed, "My Father, if it is not possible for this cup to be taken away unless I drink it, may your will be done." When he came back, he again found them sleeping, because their eyes were heavy. So he left them and went away once more and prayed the third time, saying the same thing.

Matthew 26:36–44 (NIV)

In the above verses, we come to the time immediately before Jesus's accusers will capture Him, lead Him to stand a mockery of a trail in front of Pontius Pilate, and ultimately hang Him on a cross to watch Him suffer and die. In these verses, we find Jesus in the Garden of Gethsemane, a place He went often to pray and speak with his Father. Jesus knew what was ahead of Him. He knew He would be tortured, beaten, and crucified. In the garden, Jesus felt the weight of the sin of the world that was being laid upon Him, the sin of every person past, present, and future. In Luke 22:44 (NIV), it says about Jesus, "And being in anguish, he prayed more earnestly, and his sweat was like drops of blood falling to the ground." What horrific torture the Son of God endured and faced for us. Jesus went through it all so we could be forgiven of our sins, so we could be in eternity with Jesus and the Father, and so we could live a life of joy, peace, and hope that God promised us.

What is most telling in this text is that Jesus not once but three times pleaded with the Father that if it was possible, to take this cup from Him. But He added, "Yet not as I will, but as you will" (Matthew 26:39, NIV). Even though Jesus was the Son of God and was perfect, He was still man in human form. He still knew pain and agony, hurt and sorrow, fatigue and exhaustion. Jesus experienced all the same feelings we experience. I can only imagine the fear He must have felt. In his humanity, Jesus asked His Father to stop what was about to happen. But even in this darkest hour, knowing the horror that was ahead of Him, Jesus ultimately accepted that it was not for Him to decide what was going to happen. He knew that God was in total control of the situation. Jesus knew He came to earth to be the living sacrifice for all mankind. Even in His agony Jesus still said, "May your will be done" (Matthew 26:42, NIV).

When I picture this scene in my mind, I am often brought to tears. When I think of what Jesus was about to suffer and yet He still said your will and not mine, I am overwhelmed by the sacrifice He made for you and me. I think about the many times I have tried to take control of a situation, make my own choices, and leave God entirely out of the equation. By not including God, I was saying I knew better than God and that I could handle my life on my own. I was wrong. We can go through life without God if we choose to, but our life will ultimately end up in shambles. We need God to direct us in everything we do. We need to have the courage that Jesus had in the garden. We need to be able to say to our Father, "Your will and not mine."

According to the Anxiety and Depression Association of America, 40 million adults in the United States over the age of eighteen suffer from some sort of anxiety disorder. That is 18.1 percent of the population of the United States. It's a staggering number, to say the least. I was one of those 40 million adults. The chances that you or one of your loved ones also suffers from anxiety is highly probable. I believe and understand that there are people who suffer from anxiety and depression from a chemical imbalance in their bodies, and the only way to overcome that imbalance is through medication and the help of the medical profession. I also believe that many people are like me—overburdened, overwhelmed, overscheduled, and struggling to control every aspect of their lives. They're jamming their schedules so full that they never have time to just sit down and relax. Maybe like me, they find it incredibly difficult to relax, so they do everything they can to not attempt what seems like an impossible feat. Maybe they strive for perfection in everything they do.

While striving for perfection is not a terrible thing, the weight of the pressure and self-deprecation that often comes with it can become an incredibly heavy burden to carry.

I do not remember when my anxiety first started, and I do not remember a time I lived without it in some form or another. Through the worst trials of my life, my anxiety was the greatest. I had terrible stomach issues that went undiagnosed for years. There were times the only food I could manage to digest was rice and oatmeal. The worse my anxiety was, the worse my stomach was. Sleepless nights, weight loss, chest pains, and headaches were just some of the effects of the anxiety that filled my body. For years I never sought help for my anxiety because I thought it made me seem weak. Instead, I pushed it aside as best I could. I just learned to live with it. Then, as my relationship with the Lord grew, I finally found my tool for fighting anxiety. I learned to fight it with the Word of God. For me, filling my mind with the Word of God and His promises helped me deal with my anxiety for the first time in my life. I knew that because of His love for me and His promises, I did not need to live a life filled with fear or worry anymore. If I could be like Jesus and surrender completely to God, telling Him "your will, not mine," I could find an inner peace that could help calm the anxiety I had battled for so long.

Fear and worry are mentioned hundreds of times in the Bible. In fact, by some accounts, the phrase "fear not" is used 365 times. That is one time for each day of the year. Clearly, God understood that fear and worry would be something that would plague men and women greatly, and He wanted to help us battle those fears. Jesus says:

> Therefore I tell you, do not worry about your life, what you will eat or drink; or about your body, what you will wear. Is not life more than food, and the body more than clothes? Look at the birds of the air; they do not sow or reap or store away in barns, and yet your heavenly Father feeds them. Are you not much more valuable than they? Can any one of you by worrying add a single hour to your life?
>
> Matthew 6:25–26 (NIV)

Jesus clearly understood worry. In these verses, He wants us to understand that if the Father provides for the birds in the air, then of course He will provide for His children. We must have faith in the Father that He will provide for all our needs. Worry and fear are the opposite of faith.

The Merriam-Webster dictionary defines faith as "belief and trust in and loyalty to God." When we have faith in God, we trust and believe in His promises, enduring love, and what He has planned for us. As we grow in our faith and begin our journey with the Lord, we will pass through many stages of development. In the beginning of our journey with the Lord, we will simply be like an infant who expects God to just give us what we ask for. As we grow in our relationship with the Lord, we will begin to understand that God is not a vending machine. He has His timing and His plan, and it is always good and perfect.

As our faith grows, we learn to trust God's timing and plan. We start to not worry about everything but to cast our worries on Him. 1 Peter 5:7 (NLT) tells us, "Give all your worries and cares to God, for he cares about you." God wants us to give

Him all our worries, not just a few or some of them. He wants every single one of them, no matter how small or large. He wants to carry those worries for us because He cares for us and loves us that much.

As we continue to walk with the Lord, we must come to a time in our life when we surrender to God as Jesus did in the Garden of Gethsemane. We must realize that to have true peace and contentment, we need to do as Jesus did and tell God, "Your will and not mine." Sounds scary, right? It is not at all. When you finally surrender and give control of your life to Jesus and say, "Your will, your way," it will be one of the most freeing experiences of your life. If you are like me who happens to have controlling tendencies, you will need great resolve to just let go. It will not be easy at first, but the more you let go and give *everything* over to Him, you will find more peace and start to understand what it truly means to rest in God.

When we give everything to God, we can let go of our anxieties and worries. We must remember that we do have an enemy who is going to do everything he can to keep us filled with worry, fear, and anxiety. Once we understand that worry is not of God but of the enemy, we can dismiss our worries and cast them on our Lord as soon as they appear. That is when memorization of Bible verses is so important. As soon as I start to feel overwhelmed and anxiety starts to take over, I recall the words of God and repeat them over and over—out loud if I can, and if not, in my mind. Some of my favorite verses to repeat are Matthew 11:28–30 (NIV), "Come to me, all you who are weary and burdened, and I will give you rest. Take my yoke upon you and learn from me, for I am gentle and humble in heart, and you will find rest for your souls. For my yoke is easy and my burden is light." It calms my heart and fills my soul to know that Jesus will give us rest and that He wants us to take His yoke (a wooden piece of farm equipment that joins animals together so they can pull a load equally).

Another way I often deal with my anxiety is to simply say, "Your will, your way, Father." When I find myself getting ready to make a rash decision, I whisper to myself, "Your will, Your way, my faith." That reminds me that through my faith, I trust the Lord completely and let Him guide every choice I make. I need to slow down and ask God what He wants me to do first. If it is a big decision and I need to give someone an answer, I often say, "I need to pray on it, and I will get back to you." That gives me time to clear my thoughts and not jump to a quick decision on my own. It allows me ask God what He wants me to do. It is amazing when we ask God what He wants us to do how the next morning a clear answer is on our heart, and we know what direction to go. God wants to help us and guide us. He does not want us to walk our life here alone. He wants us to lean on Him.

While we will never have to endure the immense pain and suffering that Jesus did in the garden when he cried out to the Father, we can learn so much from Jesus if we give up and surrender ourselves completely to God as He did. We need to let God take control of our lives. Because of our human nature, it is not always easy. There will be times that you will doubt what God's will is. There will be times when you question Him and wonder if it is God you are hearing or yourself. There will be times that you will not do what He wants you to. That is okay, and God understands. After all, He created us. When we slip and fall, we must get back up again, repent, and get on with doing what God wants us to do. I promise that once you learn to tell God "your will, your way, Father," your life will change. He will lead you to more amazing things than you could ever imagine. You will begin a journey with the greatest captain of all time guiding the ship, and you will finally begin to be able to let go of all your anxieties and worries and rest in the peace of your loving Father.

CHAPTER 10

Miracles Can Happen

As Jesus was walking along, he saw a man who had been blind from birth. "Rabbi," his disciples asked him, "why was this man born blind? Was it because of his own sins or his parents' sins?"

"It was not because of his sins or his parents' sins," Jesus answered. "This happened so the power of God could be seen in him. We must quickly carry out the tasks assigned us by the one who sent us. The night is coming, and then no one can work. But while I am here in the world, I am the light of the world."

Then he spit on the ground, made mud with the saliva, and spread the mud over the blind man's eyes. He told him, "Go wash yourself in the pool of Siloam" (Siloam means "sent"). So, the man went and washed and came back seeing!

John 9:1–7 (NLT)

In the first four books of the New Testament (Matthew, Mark, Luke, and John), also known as the four Gospels, we find many accounts of the miracles Jesus preformed during His three-year ministry leading up to His crucifixion. In fact, many of these stories are familiar to those who are not familiar with the

Bible—the feeding of the 5,000, the healing of the blind man and the leper, Jesus turning water into wine, and Jesus walking on water. They are all accounts that many have heard in Sunday morning Bible school as a child. Jesus was God incarnate, the light of the world, the bread of life, the healer, the Savior, perfection. Jesus came to heal the blind, to make the lame walk, and to raise the dead. Many ask if these same miracles that Jesus performed more than 2,000 years ago with His own hands are available to us today. Can God perform miracles here on earth now? Yes, He can. I am living proof.

Not long after my kidney was removed in 1979, my mother discovered another health issue. While changing my diaper one day, she saw something strange protruding out of me, and then it disappeared. My mother has told me many times that she thought she had lost her mind until a nurse saw the same thing during a follow-up visit for my kidney removal. The doctors at Johns Hopkins ran some tests on me and discovered that I had a condition called a ureterocele. As defined by the Cleveland Clinic (https://my.clevelandclinic.org/health/diseases/16322-ureterocele), "Ureteroceles are birth defects that happen during the prenatal period. The ends of the ureter that enter the bladder do not develop properly. The ureterocele blocks the flow of urine. The defect can be found before birth. Treatment depends on when the defect is discovered."

Normally there are not any visible symptoms of a ureterocele, so the issue can go undetected for a long period of time. In the late 1970s, medical technology was a far cry from the standards of today. At that time, many ureteroceles went undiscovered, and the damage to a child's kidneys could be great, even deadly. Following the discovery of my ureterocele, the doctors told my parents that I would need another surgery around my first birthday to remove the blockage. The surgery would be as difficult as the kidney removal that I was still recovering from. Fear filled my parents as they imagined me undergoing another surgery in less than a year. The fear and dread of the impending surgery took precedence over the oddity of this situation that there was no real explanation for what my mother or the nurse had seen that had led to my diagnosis. Now we know that it was the start of the miracle God would work in this seemingly implausible situation.

Several weeks passed, and one afternoon my mother and grandmother decided to go have lunch in a small neighboring town at a local chicken shop called English's. While my mother was at the counter paying, she noticed my grandmother talking to an unfamiliar woman. Back in those days, the Eastern Shore of Maryland was like the TV show *Cheers* where everyone knew your name, so it was unusual to see someone unfamiliar. My mother grew concerned as she saw my grandmother hand me over to the woman. That was extremely unusual behavior for my very overprotective grandmother, so my mother went back to investigate the situation. My grandmother explained that this woman had approached her out of the clear blue and asked if I had been ill. My grandmother told the stranger about the surgery I had just gone through and the upcoming surgery. While still holding me, the woman asked, "May I pray over your daughter?" and then she did. She handed me back and left as quickly as she came. My mother and grandmother never got her name, and they never saw her again.

Several months went by, and I returned to Johns Hopkins for a checkup and to see if the blockage had increased. The doctors had planned to prepare for the next steps of the impending surgery. The urologist ran another battery of tests. After some time, he informed my parents of something astonishing. The ureterocele had simply disappeared. Just as there was no explanation for the events that led to the discovery of my condition, there was also no explanation for its disappearance. The urologist, who was considered one of the leading urologists in the world at the time and had performed my kidney surgery, explained it simply to my mother. "Mrs. Showell, we see miracles here all the time. Your daughter is one of those miracles."

My parents continued to take me to Johns Hopkins for checkups for many years. The ureterocele never reappeared, and I never had to have the second surgery. I went on to grow strong and healthy. God performed a miracle in my young life. He answered the prayers of not just my mother, my father, and other family members but of a kind stranger who helped me be blessed beyond measure.

Miracles are around us every day, some small, some immense. The changing of a cold hard winter into a beautiful, bountiful spring is a miracle. The birth of a child is a miracle. When you are running late for work and miss a terrible accident by mere minutes, that is a miracle. Miracles are all around us. We just have to take the time to see them and realize them for what they are.

God can bring a miracle to you, too, through a stranger or someone you may never expect. Maybe the miracle is something you prayed for long ago and forgot about. Then when the timing is right, God opens that door for the miracle to happen. God told the prophet Jeremiah, "I am the Lord the God of all the peoples of the world. Is anything too hard for me?" (Jeremiah 32:27, NLT). Nothing is too hard for God. Nothing is impossible. We must stop focusing on what we think is impossible in the flesh and pray and focus on God who makes all things possible.

My grandfather—or Pop-Pop as I called him—died when I was just four years old. My mother's father was the type of man some people call the salt of the earth. He was kind and humble and would do anything for anyone. He worked hard as a waterman to provide for his family. He tonged oysters for a living. In other words, he went out on his boat in the cold, bitter, winter and used huge metal tongs to dredge up oysters from the bottom of the bay and then sell them at market. It was not the easiest of livings, to say the least. Pop-Pop was an active member of the little community he lived in. He had been saved in the later years of his life through a local pastor, right in the dining room of my grandparents' house. He and the man who led him to Jesus, Reverend Huffman, became close friends. Reverend Huffman performed the funeral service for my grandfather when he passed of a heart attack at just fifty-nine years of age. While my Pop-Pop had not accepted Jesus as his Savior until much later in his life, the miracle that happened to him shows that even though you might not know God personally, God always knows you.

It was the mid 1960s, and my grandparents lived in a quaint home in the small fishing town of Neavitt, Maryland. They owned a miniature pinscher named Tiny at the time. One night, late in the evening, my grandfather went to let Tiny outside to do his duty. It was dark, and my grandfather fell, landing on the concrete sidewalk and fracturing his skull. My mother, who was only 16, found him on the sidewalk. He was rushed to the hospital. After about a week in the hospital, my Pop-Pop's face began to draw up much like someone who has suffered facial paralysis after a stroke. He could not drink out of a straw without the liquids of his drink pouring out of his mouth. The doctors said his face would remain like that the rest of his life. He was just 40 years old.

Neavitt was like many small towns at that time, small on population but mighty in faith. Word spread fast about my grandfather's fall and injury. The churches in the town began adding him to their prayer lists, and the locals began praying for him. Then one morning about three months later, my grandfather awoke to find that something astounding had happened. Overnight, his face had been healed. The prayers of a little community had been answered. His face returned to normal. God had placed His mighty hand on my Pop-Pop, and not only had God healed him, but my Pop-Pop would be a testimony I would share with you more than 50 years later. It is a testimony that no matter how small your faith is, God can work miracles. Jesus said in Matthew 17:20 (NIV), "Truly I tell you, if you have faith as small as a mustard seed, you can say to this mountain, 'Move from here to there,' and it will move. Nothing will be impossible for you." The faith of a tiny mustard seed—a faith that might be small, but a faith that is mighty and can do anything.

I have the testimony of two amazing physical miracles. Sometimes miracles are as much unseen as they are seen. When I look back at what I have endured in my life, the hurt and abuse that I have recovered from, the doors that have opened and closed, the beauty that God has allowed me to see, I realize that each one of these events is a miracle of its own, made by God's hand. As I stated in earlier chapters, God always keeps His promise to work everything out for the good of those who love Him and are called according to His purpose (see Romans 8:28). I believe this with every part of my being. What we must understand is that God works everything out according to His plan and His timing, not ours.

Take a deep breath, and look back at your life. I realize that not everyone has had a physical healing like mine, but I can guarantee you that if you think long and hard about it, you will see that God has been working in your life all along, performing miracles along the way. Realizing and thanking God for the miracles He has already worked in your life will help open the door for you to trust that He will answer more seemingly impossible prayers.

Have you been praying for something that seems impossible? God specializes in the impossible. Do you need something to happen fast, like a new job before you have no funds left in the bank? Do you feel like you have many dreams but are not sure they will ever come to fruition? Do you wonder every day what you can do? Talk to God, pray, repent for your mistakes, ask for forgiveness, and ask God to help you and provide the miracle you so desperately seek.

"Jesus looked at them and said, 'With man it is impossible, but not with God. For all things are possible with God'" (Mark 10:27, ESV). Notice that Jesus did not say some things; He said all things. God can make anything happen if it is His will. As we ask God to help us, we need to make sure we pray with gratitude and thank God for what He has done and what He is going to do. Remember to always pray, "If it is your will, Father" (Chapter 9). As hard as it might be to understand, we should only want what is God's will for our life. God knows our life like a book, except He knows it from the end back to the beginning. Because God is almighty and all-knowing, His will is so much greater than our own.

It is true that not every prayer will be answered. Not everyone will receive the miracle they are asking for. You might know someone who was miraculously healed from cancer while your own parent died from the same horrible disease. Maybe you have had an unanswered prayer for years and do not understand why God has not answered it when you see prayers around being answered for others. I wish I had an explanation, but I do not. No one does. That is just one of the mysterious things about our Lord.

There are answers we will not understand while we are here on earth. What we must realize is that God does have a reason why some miracles happen and others do not. We live our life moving forward, but many times we see it backward, realizing after the fact why something did not happen and why it was best that it did not. Other times, especially when it comes to the death of a loved one, our loss is one of the pains of life we must endure. While our prayers for their healing and survival might not have been answered, we must remember that the love you shared with them during their life was a gift, a blessing, and a miracle all wrapped in one.

Before your feet hit the floor each morning, take a moment to ask God to let you see all the miracles that surround you each day. Ask Him to open your eyes to all the blessings that happen each day in the world. Focus on the good in the world that God is creating and the good that is happening in your life. No matter how small that good might be, if you have faith—the faith of a mustard seed—you can move mountains, and our mighty God can create that miracle you have been waiting for.

CHAPTER 11

Learning to Love Again, God's Way

If I could speak all the languages of earth and of angels, but didn't love others, I would only be a noisy gong or a clanging cymbal. If I had the gift of prophecy, and if I understood all of God's secret plans and possessed all knowledge, and if I had such faith that I could move mountains, but didn't love others, I would be nothing. If I gave everything I have to the poor and even sacrificed my body, I could boast about it; but if I did not love others, I would have gained nothing.

Love is patient and kind. Love is not jealous or boastful or proud or rude. It does not demand its own way. It is not irritable, and it keeps no record of being wronged. It does not rejoice about injustice but rejoices whenever the truth wins out. Love never gives up, never loses faith, is always hopeful, and endures through every circumstance".

1 Corinthians 13:1–7 (NLT)

Many consider 1 Corinthians 13 the love chapter of the Bible. The Apostle Paul describes to us what love is and what it is not. He tells us that above everything we have, if we do not have love, then we have nothing at all. The word *love* is mentioned in the New International Version of the Bible 574 times. In the

Gospel of John, the word *love* (in all forms) appears 57 times. In the book of Mark, Jesus tells us this:

> The most important commandment is this: "Listen, O Israel! The LORD our God is the one and only LORD. And you must love the LORD your God with all your heart, all your soul, all your mind, and all your strength." The second is equally important: "Love your neighbor as yourself." No other commandment is greater than these.
>
> Mark 12:29–31 (NLT)

Love was the focus of Jesus's ministry. Love is clearly extremely important to God, but why? Because God is love—perfect love. God's love is unending, unchanging, and unwavering. God loves us not because of what we do or who we are. He loves us because of who He is. Nothing we can ever do can stop God from loving us. He will never love you any more or any less than He loves you today. His love is as wide as the east is from the west. God loves each of us and wants us to love Him and each other in the same way.

God gave us free will so we would make the choice to love Him. He did not want to force us to love Him. He wants us to have a relationship with Him. He wants us to love Him with all our being. He wants to be number one in our lives. Jesus said that loving one another is as equally important to loving God. You are to "love your neighbor as you love yourself." I would say most people find that to be one of the most challenging verses in the Bible. I know it is for me. It is something I struggle with daily. To love your neighbor is to love everyone, no matter who they are or what they may have done. That means you cannot just love the lovable people in your life. You must love the person who cut you off on the expressway, the grouchy relative who always wants to argue politics with you at the Thanksgiving dinner table, and the person from your past who hurt you to your core.

In the English language, we use the word *love* in many contexts. We can love our new car, our dog, our husband, our mom, and that new flavored coffee at the local coffee shop. Surely, we do not "love" all these things in the same way. Originally, the New Testament was written in Greek. The Greek language has four words that make up our one English word *love*. The words are *storge*, *philia*, *eros*, and *agape*. Storge is the type of love shared in families, a familiar love like between a parent and a child. Philia is a love or bond between friends. Think of the name of the city of Philadelphia, "the city of brotherly love." Eros is passionate or romantic love. Finally, agape is godly love, true unconditional love not based on certain feelings or emotions. It's a self-sacrificing love.

Understanding that these four words were used by the writers of the New Testament to describe love helps us have a deeper understanding of what love is. God does not expect us to love everyone equally or in the same form, but He does expect us to love everyone. God knows that we cannot love everyone without His help, and He knows we are going to stumble and falter.

Notice in the above verses that Jesus says you are to "love your neighbor as yourself." We must love ourselves before we can even begin to love everyone around us. As we discussed in earlier chapters of this book, the first step is to understand that God loves you unconditionally. Through that understanding, you can love your own self completely just as God created you. After that, we can start the journey along with God to help us find love for ourselves from relationships and begin the lifelong process of loving others the way Jesus does.

After two failed marriages, learning to love myself was hard enough, but the thought of loving someone again seemed impossible. Like most people, I had always thought I was supposed to fall in love. Rick Warren, author of *The Purpose Driven Life*, says we don't fall in love. He says that is like tripping and falling into a ditch. I still laugh when I think about that and how I certainly fell into a ditch with love a time or two. I am guessing that many of you have as well. What most of us do not realize is that love is a choice. It is a decision we make every day when we wake up. Am I going to choose to love today and spread love to everyone as Jesus did? Or am I going to be a bitter, angry, miserable person? I chose for a long time to be a bitter, angry, miserable person. I believed that if I did not choose to love, then I would be able to protect myself from the hurt and pain that had riddled my heart time and time again from past relationships. What I did not realize was that by closing myself off and choosing not to love, I was essentially closing myself off from receiving the amazing love that comes from our heavenly Father. Love is like a door. If you close the door and lock it, you make it not only impossible for you to get out but also for anything else to get in. While God loves us unconditionally, if we want to know God's love, we must open our hearts to be able to receive it. When we harden our hearts so much that we choose not to give love, we also choose not to accept it, whether we realize it or not.

I am not sure what event in my life caused me to shut the door to my heart. Maybe it was the pain from the loss of my father, the abuse from my first husband, or the incredible hurt and disappointment caused by choices people made who said they loved me. Maybe it was the pain from the betrayal of being cheated on and lied to. Maybe it was from the sense of failure I carried as I watched one relationship after another fail. Or maybe it was the firm belief I carried that I was simply not good enough for anyone to love.

Whichever of those events started it, the day my second husband walked out of my life after eleven years was when I slammed shut the door of love. I remember vividly how he stood at the back door of our home preparing to leave and said, "I don't believe you ever truly loved me." He believed this because I had made the conscious choice to not have children with him. While his reasoning was incorrect (I had never wanted children), I look back and think that his statement, while devastating to hear, was probably true.

It certainly was not that I had not tried to love him. It was that once again I had fallen "in the ditch of love" when I met him. I was enamored with the thought of love. I was trying to make right all the wrongs I had made in prior relationships. I was trying to fill that empty hole in my heart that longed for approval. What I did not understand was that no human could ever provide what I needed. Only God could. I did not understand that I could not make the choice to love someone if I did not understand what true, perfect love is—love from the Father. I love the verse from 1 John 4:18 (NLT) that says, "Such love has no fear, because perfect love expels all fear. If we are afraid, it is for fear of punishment, and this shows that we have not fully experienced his perfect love." Perfect love is what we receive from our Savior, Jesus Christ. It is the only place we can receive it.

Without knowing His love, we often walk in fear and cannot make the choice to love anyone. As much as I wanted and believed I loved my second husband, he was probably correct. Neither he nor I understood what it was to choose love, and without understanding it, I do not think we were ever capable of loving each other. Sadly, I believe this is the reason so many marriages fall apart. We jump into the deep end of a relationship without looking at the person we are diving in with. We do not understand the work and commitment it takes to be able to choose to love every day.

When my second husband left, I consciously made the choice that I would never trust or love again. At the age of thirty-five, I had given up. The words "I have had enough, I will not ever let that happen to me again" were what I held on to. Have you muttered those same or similar words? If you have, you and I have stood on the same precipice. We have tottered on the edge of the cliff of self-destruction and self-defeat, not understanding or knowing that without love, life is nothing. Remember what the Apostle Paul said in 1 Corinthians 13:3 (NIV), "[If I] do not have love, I gain nothing." Without love, we will become bitter and burned out. Instead of protecting ourselves, we will destroy ourselves unknowingly. What we need to understand is that no matter how lost, how hurt, or how broken we become because of humans, God's love, His perfect unwavering love, is all we need. Through understanding and receiving God's love, we can and will learn to love again but this time in His way, not ours.

Over the next year, I tried hard to hold the door to my heart shut, but God's unfailing love made that impossible. Seven months after my second husband's departure, I fully committed my life to walking with and serving Jesus. I have often thought back to that time in my life and thanked God for His amazing plans and how His hand was on my life even though I did not realize it. I now know that if my second husband, who did not believe in Jesus or God, had stayed in my life, I may have never found Jesus the way I did. As I have stated earlier in this book. I had always known Jesus as my Savior and had prayed on and off in my life, but I had never committed myself to Jesus, nor did I understand what having Jesus in my life meant. Through what I thought was a horrible loss, I gained the most important relationship I could ever have—my relationship with Christ. Now I was choosing to love the One who would love me no matter what I did or who I was. I was choosing to love the One who had died for me, who had paid the ultimate price. I chose to love Jesus.

Over the next months, I began to ask God if He would put someone in my life—when He was ready—that I could build a relationship with. I asked for someone I could trust, who would be honest and faithful, hardworking, and a man who loved his family and God. I asked for a man I could finally build a life with. Just five months later, God put that man in my life.

When I first met Kevin, I admit that I was still a mess in many ways. I was overwhelmed by the job I had, and I was not the happiest person. I had severe trust issues and still was not completely open to the fact that I would ever find someone who would love me and accept me for who I was. God was changing me, but that change was going to take time. Now

I realize that in our relationship with the Lord, we will keep changing throughout our entire life here on earth. He will keep molding us and shaping us, just like a potter does with clay. He will continue the process of developing our character until the day He finally calls us home. To help us in this changing process, He must often bring certain people into our lives. I know that is what He did with Kevin.

Kevin and I had both been hurt a lot in many ways by others, so it was hard for both of us to see past the hurt. I prayed diligently that God would heal both of our hearts. I prayed these verses: "The Lord is near the broken hearted and saves the crushed in spirit" (Psalm 34:18, ESV) and "Therefore, if anyone is in Christ, the new creation has come: The old has gone, the new is here!" (2 Corinthians 5:17, NIV). I believed with all my heart that God had the power to heal all the wounds that were deeply rooted in both of us and that through Him, my soul and spirit that had been crushed more times than I could count would finally be healed. As I prayed these verses, I knew that I was a new creation because of my acceptance and understanding of Christ as my Savior. I was like an onion, and Jesus would have to peel away the layers of the old in order for the new to begin to shine through. I was slowly letting go of the door I had been so determined to hold shut. God was filling me with His amazing, pure love, and it was showing me that I no longer had to walk in fear of what had been. I was to walk with strength and courage of what would be because God was walking right beside me.

I reflect and see how God's timing with my relationship with Kevin was perfect. While I was impatient and wanted things to move along, I always had a reassurance in my soul that things were working out at the right pace. Slowly, our relationship developed, and the amazing friendship we had created blossomed into what love is supposed to be—patient and kind, not jealous or boastful, a love that will endure. It was a love that was easy. Relationships will not always be easy, but the pure, true love that a relationship is built on should ultimately feel easy. It should not be a great battle. It should reflect the love that God has for us, a love that is unwavering and steadfast. A love that is honest and trustworthy. A love that is not what we see on TV or read in a romantic novel. A love that is seen in God's Word.

"He heals the broken hearted and binds up their wounds" (Psalm 147:3, NIV). If you had told me years ago when I felt like my life was crumbling to the ground due to another broken relationship that I would be able to open my heart so freely to love those around me without fear, I would have told you that you were crazy. No matter how broken you are, no matter how much hurt you have had in your life, no matter what your past is, you can learn to love in the same way God loves. God does not care about the past. He loves you no matter what. God wants to heal your hurts so you can open your heart up and love Him and love others. That is really what everything comes down to. God wants us to love Him and love others. In Psalm 147:3, He promises to heal our hearts and bandage our wounds just as any loving parent would do for their child. I can testify that if you let God, He will do just that and much more.

When we understand God's love, we find a contentment that truly does pass understanding. We find a peace that lies within us that fills our hearts so full that love overflows. A love from God will teach you how to love His pure, unbiased, perfect way. The journey to love again is not an easy one. I cannot promise that God will give you an amazing personal relationship as He did for me. God's plan is different for each of us. What I do know is that God will give you people to give your love to. It might not be a husband or a wife. It might be an elderly person who is all alone, a child who has suffered from abuse, or a friend who needs the guidance and love of a sister or brother of faith. There are so many in our world who desperately need love, just as you do. Open yourself to receive the amazing gift of God's love, and soon you will be spreading that incredible gift of His love to others.

CHAPTER 12

Understanding Your Purpose, Calling, and Gifts

To everything there is a season,
and a time for every purpose under heaven:
a time to be born and a time to die,
a time to plant and a time to uproot,
a time to kill and a time to heal,
a time to break down and a time to build,
a time to weep and a time to laugh,
a time to mourn and a time to dance,
a time to cast away stones and a time to gather stones together,
a time to embrace and a time to refrain from embracing,
a time to search and a time to count as lost,
a time to keep and a time to discard,
a time to tear and a time to mend,
a time to be silent and a time to speak,
a time to love and a time to hate,
a time for war and a time for peace.

Ecclesiastes 3:1–8 (BSB)

It is no wonder that in the 1950s, songwriter Pete Seeger decided to use the first eight verses of Ecclesiastes 3 to help him pen what would become the legendary folk song, "Turn! Turn! Turn!" recorded by the American folk-rock group the Byrds in the

1960s. I have always loved these eight verses. I think about King Solomon who wrote these verses after he had been granted great wisdom by God. I wonder if he realized how these words that he wrote almost 3,000 years ago would remain so relevant and powerful today, how these eight verses perfectly sum up what each of us experience on our journeys.

What stands out to me most is what is written in verse 1, "a time for every purpose under heaven." God who created the stars and the heavens has a purpose for each individual living thing. What an amazing Father we have! This same Father who created the oceans and the mountains selected a purpose for each one of us. God created us to be unique with a particular purpose, mission, and calling.

Rick Warren's incredible book *The Purpose Driven Life*, has sold more than 50 million copies in more than 85 languages. I highly recommend either reading it or listening to it. The book is meant to be read over the course of forty days (one chapter a day). It is an amazing resource when it comes to finding and understanding what your purpose in life through God is. I could never come close to doing justice to breaking down details of your purpose in life the way *The Purpose Driven Life* does. What I can do, though, is share with you my life experiences with the unique gifts and callings God gave me.

For many years, I wondered what my purpose was. I lived in fear, worrying that somehow I might miss my purpose. I struggled to understand why God had put me here and given me life for what I was supposed to do. I felt for many years that my job must be my purpose, but I came to realize that was not the case. According to the U.S. Bureau of Labor Statistics, the average person will have twelve to fifteen jobs in their lifetime.

Certainly, your job cannot be your purpose if you will have fifteen of them. Of course, there are those whose career is their life's purpose. Even for those, life is meant to be much more than our job or career. What I had failed to realize for so long was that we do not just have one great purpose in life. We have many purposes that God gives us while we are here.

Notice again in Ecclesiastes 3:1 that the exact wording is, "To everything there is a season, a time for *every* purpose under heaven" (emphasis added). It does not say each purpose. The word *each* would refer to a single person or thing. The word *every* refers to many people or things. In every purpose, we will have multiple purposes. In *The Purpose Driven Life*, Warren shows us five purposes of our life based on biblical principles. One of those five purposes is to live out our missions here on earth. One of those missions is to follow through on what Jesus's mission was here on earth—to help bring the unsaved to the Lord, to help bring unbelievers to Jesus so they will have eternal salvation. The act of bringing someone to Jesus so they will live in eternity with Christ is the most important thing we as Christians can do. Can you imagine on the day you arrive in heaven being greeted by those who made it there because of you, because you brought the love of Jesus to them? What an amazing day that will be!

Our second mission is to spread the testimony of our lives. This mission is how the book you are reading came about. I believed that Jesus wanted me to share my life—the troubles and the trials, the miracles and the blessings, the good and the bad. Each one of us has a testimony of our life. Not everyone is going to write a book, but everyone can share with others how the Lord helped them through great struggles and adversity.

Maybe you went through a terrible financial crisis but God brought you through it to even greater prosperity on the other side. You could take your time to volunteer and encourage those who have lost their jobs and are down on their luck like you were. Maybe you survived a terribly abusive relationship. You could seek out a women's shelter and speak to other survivors of domestic abuse about how God's love changed your life. The possibilities are endless.

Even if you think you do not have a testimony, trust me, you do. We all do. That is part of our lives here on earth. In John 16:33 (NLT), Jesus said "I have told you all this so that you may have peace in me. Here on earth you will have many trials and sorrows. But take heart, because I have overcome the world." We are given trials here on earth so we can see how the goodness of God works. Then we can tell others. If everything in our lives was wonderful, we would never appreciate the goodness. We must have adversity in order to celebrate the incredible blessings God has given us. We must be tested in order to have a testimony. Our mission is to then use our testimonies to help, support, and encourage others and show them the goodness of our Savior.

We now know that God put us here on earth for multiple purposes and missions, but what about your calling? Merriam-Webster defines *calling* as "a strong inner impulse toward a particular course of action especially when accompanied by conviction of divine influence." I love that definition. Our divine influence that gives us that inner impulse is the Holy Spirit who lives inside everyone who have accepted Jesus as their Savior. What we must not be conformed to is worldly thought—that I only have one calling and if I miss that calling, I have failed. That is certainly not the case. God will keep calling us no matter how old we are or how long we have lived our life without Him. If we have breath in our body, we can follow the calling God has for us. God will keep calling us as long as we are here on earth. He wants us to serve Him and live out what He placed us here to do. He will keep calling us just as He called Samuel in the Old Testament.

The Lord called to Samuel three times (1 Samuel 3). Each time He called Samuel's name, Samuel ran to Eli, his master, the high priest. Samuel said to Eli each time, "Here I am!" and Eli would tell him he had not called him. After the third time this happened, Eli realized it was the Lord calling Samuel. He told Samuel to go lie down, and if he heard the voice of the Lord, he should say, "Speak, Lord, your servant is listening" (1 Samuel 3:9, NLT). Samuel heard God's voice again, served and obeyed Him, and became a great prophet after whom two books of the Old Testament are named.

The story of Samuel is very important because it shows us that God is not going to let you miss out on how He wants to use you. Samuel heard God call his name three times before he realized it was God calling. God will keep calling you too. He wants to use you and see you fulfill what He created you for. The problem is that many of us get so distracted by the outside world that we do not realize what God is calling us for. We focus on what we think we should be doing or what we want to do, not what God wants. Maybe you want to be a professional basketball player, but you are only five foot four and lack the hand-eye coordination it requires to compete at that level. Yet you have an amazing ability to communicate with and comfort people, and your heart becomes full when you help others.

Maybe your calling is not the NBA but to use the skills God gave you to become a social worker where you can help others. We are going to continue to be dissatisfied when we spend our lives wishing we were doing something instead of doing what God has called us to do. Your calling will fill your heart with a joy you cannot explain. You will know this is what you are meant to do at this time. We must serve the purpose of the season we are in. Just like Samuel, your calling will find you.

From the time I was a young child, my passion for dance was great. It was clear that I had a talent for dancing. It came to me very naturally. I felt the music and the motion in my soul. As a kid, I would go outside and "play" for hours just dancing around to music. Each week I could not wait for the day of my dance class so I would have the opportunity to learn how to fine-tune my skills. Many people have asked me over the years who I got the skill of dancing from. Certainly, one of my parents or relatives must have been a professional dancer. This was not the case at all. While my parents enjoyed social dancing, they were just novice dancers when I began my journey in my career of ballroom dancing at the age of nine. When I started taking ballet at six years of age, no one in my family danced. I had inherited the talent of dance, but that gift came down from my heavenly Father, not my earthly one. God gave me the gift and talent for dance. In turn, He took that talent and gave me the gift of competitiveness, which drove me to have a successful amateur and professional career. Out of the gift of competitiveness was birthed a successful competitive career. He gave me the gift and talent to teach dance, which I would use to bring joy into people's lives during the next season of my life.

The ability to dance would also bring forth another gift our Lord had blessed me with, the ability to raise money for nonprofit organizations, which was revealed because of a fundraiser I chaired based on dancing. This was yet another season of my life. Through the gift of the ability to fundraise, God brought another calling into my life for another season, the job of executive director of a humane society. God's gifts of a soft heart for animals in need, good organizational and planning skills, and the knack of getting people to donate money all led me to that job when I had no prior experience. It came completely out of the blue. I could go on and on about how God let one gift or skill He blessed me with lead to the next opportunity and then the next. This is how our God works, laying one stone at a time and taking us from one season to the next. Calling to calling. Glory to glory. All while serving Him along the way.

We all have different callings at different times. God takes us through each season of our life, and many times we have a different calling for each season. We can also serve multiple callings at one time. You can be called to be a wife, a mom, and a schoolteacher all at the same time during the same season. Each of those callings serves the greater good. As we go through the seasons of our lives, God can very well change what we are called to do at any moment. In my life, I went from being a dance teacher to an executive director, back to a dance teacher and a business owner, and now to being an author. While for me these callings are occupational, I believe that God has called me in many other ways. He has called me as a mentor, a foster mom for dogs, a comforter for friends, and a support and strength for my loved ones. What I did not realize long ago was that while I was looking for my great purpose in life, I was already fulfilling it. I was letting God take me from season to season, glory to glory, and answering His callings on my life, whether I realized it at the time or not.

If you are still not sure what your calling is at this moment in your life, take some time to step back and be still. Psalm 46:10 (NIV) says, "Be still and know that I am God." Being still does not mean sitting back and doing nothing. Being still means letting go and letting God take control. Let Him show you what He wants from you. Take time to write a list of things you are good at and then a list of things you enjoy. Look at both lists, and compare what things are on both lists. What brings your heart joy and happens to be what you are good at? That might be what God is calling you to do at this time. Take some time to just be quiet and let God speak to you through His Spirit.

Remember Samuel? He was lying down, resting, when God called him. If our minds are constantly filled with chatter and cluttered thoughts, you are going to have a hard time hearing God. Take time to sit in the presence of God. Tell God you are here and that you are ready to do His will, not your own. Remember, you must be truly willing to accept what God wants for you, not what you think God should want from you. Let God show you. Use the gifts, talents, abilities, and passions the Lord gave you as tools for fulfilling your calling in each season you go through in life. When you begin to live your life this way, you will start to understand the contentment the Apostle Paul spoke of in Philippians 4:12 (NIV): "I know what it is to be in need, and I know what it is to have plenty. I have learned the secret of being content in any and every situation, whether well fed or hungry, whether living in plenty or in want." No matter what season you go through, when you are walking with the Lord, serving Him, and fulfilling the calling He has for you at the time, you will know the contentment of serving your Savior and will have the peace that passes all understanding.

CHAPTER 13

Letting Him Use You

Do not conform to the pattern of this world, but be transformed by the renewing of your mind. Then you will be able to test and approve what God's will is—his good, pleasing and perfect will.

Romans 12:2 (NIV)

In Romans 12:2, the Apostle Paul is writing a letter to the Christian church in Rome. He is telling them not to follow the patterns and ways of this world but be transformed, changed, by the renewing of their minds. How do we renew our minds? We focus not on what is of this world such as TV and social media but on the ways of Christ. We do this by reading and studying the Bible, memorizing scripture, listening to sermons, enjoying Christian music, and avoiding toxic things that will pollute our minds. When our minds are focused on God, He will show us His perfect will, and we will be able walk in the path He has set forth for each of us.

In Chapter 12, we discussed understanding and finding our purpose, mission, and callings. At the end of the chapter, we looked at truly being willing to accept what God wants from us. This is such an important thing to understand when you decided to commit yourself to serving Jesus and walking in His will. As we allow ourselves to be transformed by the renewing of our minds and grow spiritually, we must understand that in order to do God's will, we must be willing to accept His will for our lives completely. To follow God's will for your life is not always easy, and at times it can be terrifying. Our faith and trust in God must trump our fear of not knowing what lies ahead.

When I decided I would give up the battle I had been fighting for more than a year, I was executive director of the animal shelter. I had prayed and asked God many times to show me what He wanted me to do in this situation. I felt the Lord speak to me through my inner spirit that it was time to let go of this job and move on. I had no idea what I would move on to. I had no idea how I would replace the salary I was making. Letting go and moving on were the last things I wanted to do. I am not the type of person to quit or surrender, and that was exactly what I felt like I was doing. I was giving up everything I had worked so hard to create. I was walking away from the animals I so loved. I was leaving behind a staff who depended on me. I knew that leaving my position meant severing ties that would never be mended, losing people I thought were my friends, and starting over again. I was filled with fear and trepidation.

Yet in all my hesitation, I knew deep down what God's will was for me. Very few people knew that I was considering leaving my position, but those who did, while they supported my decision, felt like I was letting the other side win. I felt I was letting them win as well, but I knew what God was telling me to do, so I penned the letter that would be my resignation. I would follow what I believed was God's will for me. The day I resigned was like a day of rebirth. All the hesitation I had felt was gone. All the worries I had lamented over for months disappeared. Over the next weeks and months, I saw that by following God's will for my life, no matter how hard it was initially, there were blessings that would make the doubts that once wreaked havoc in my mind disappear far into the past. God's will was just as He promised, good and perfect.

About a year after I resigned, I sat down and told God that from now on, whatever His will was for my life was the way it would be. I was all in 100 percent. As we saw in Chapter 9, it was "His will, His way, my faith." Whatever He asked of me I would do. It has not always been easy, and of course, there are times I still feel like I am not sure what God wants me to do. I get impatient wanting things to happen in my time. Then I remember 2 Peter 3:9 (ESV): "The Lord is not slow to fulfill his promise as some count slowness, but is patient toward you, not wishing that any should perish, but that all should reach repentance." This verse reminds me that God's timing is perfect and that He is in control. Every day I pray that God will show me His will and His way for my life. Of course, I ask God for things in my prayers, but I always ask that He only give them to me if that is His will and to never give me anything that would take Him from being first place in my life. I tell God that I understand it is His timing and not mine.

I have lived the path of my own choices and decisions and tried to control everything and force everything. That did not work out so great. I made horrible choices, and I lived a life full of constant worry and anxiety. Now I let God take control, and I rest in His peace. I am human, so I still worry. I still try to control things, and I still have anxiety, but I have come so far from where I was. I am growing and changing with the Lord. I always will be until I am called home, and that is okay by me. I now understand that to do God's will, I must let God change me. God wants each of us to grow to become more and more like His Son, Jesus. That is His ultimate will for each of our lives, and He is with us every step of the way as we become new in Him.

Are you ready to let God use you? Are you ready to let go of what you think you need to do and let God show you what He wants you to do? God created each of us individually. We each have our own fingerprints, our own personality, and our own voice. God's plan for your life is unique; it is His plan just for you. It is wonderful to have people to look up to, to have as your mentor, and to give you guidance and advice. But it is important to remember that you are not to emulate anyone. God has His unique plan for you. Do not envy someone else's blessings, talents, and gifts.

Be grateful and thankful for your own gifts and talents. Tell God you are ready, ready for His will and not your own. That does not mean you cannot have dreams or desires. That does not mean you cannot ask God for things. God wants us to ask Him for things. Jesus spoke many times about asking God for what you need and want. In Luke 11:9 (ESV), Jesus says, "And I tell you, ask, and it will be given to you; seek, and you will find; knock, and it will be opened to you." If God does not give you what you ask for, it is simply not His will. God's plans and dreams for our lives are so much greater than ours. Often that unanswered prayer is because He has something much greater in store for you.

My greatest hope for you is that you will take the chance to surrender yourself completely to the will of God. You will not regret it. I haven't. Surrendering to God's will for your life and letting Him use you is the greatest thing you can do to be you bravely. The you that you have been looking for, the purpose, the mission, the calling are all found in God's will for you. Walking with God, totally trusting Him, and giving yourself to Him 100 percent is being brave and strong in a way that will change your life completely.

CHAPTER 14

What the Future Has in Store

"For I know the plans I have for you," says the Lord "They are plans for good and not for disaster, to give you a future and a hope."

Jeremiah 29:11 (NLT)

For many people, their past is the one thing that is holding them back from the potential and the future the Lord has in store for them. It could have been years of abuse, heartache, or loss that is keeping you living in the past and unable to move on to the life God wants you to live. No matter what the cause, living in the past will only hinder your growth and stop you from reaching your full potential of what God wants you to become now and in the future.

The enemy is clever. He knows if he keeps reminding you of past hurts and past mistakes, you will continue to mull over these thoughts in your mind. You will start to doubt yourself and start thinking that you are incapable of moving on or having more in your life. Once we start to have this mindset, the enemy has won. Instead of falling into the enemy's trap, we must remember God's promises such as the one in Jeremiah 29:11. He promises us good plans, plans that will give us hope, plans that will give us a future. God does not promise to take away all your suffering, but He does promise you hope amid it all. It is a hope that what He has planned for your future is so much greater than what you could have ever dreamed of. We can trust in the Lord that no matter what lies behind us, we should only look forward to what lies in front of us. Our past does not determine our future. God wants us to get our hopes up and believe that He is working out something better in our lives than what we have today.

In the book of Esther is a story of a beautiful Israelite woman who becomes the queen of Persia during a time when the Israelites are held there as slaves. Esther learns of a plan by one of the king's officials to exterminate all the Israelites in the kingdom. She bravely presents herself to the king, breaking the law of the land by revealing herself as an Israelite and risking her own life in the process. Esther's great risk and sacrifice ultimately saves the entire nation of her people from being killed. In Esther 4:14 (ESV), Mordecai (Esther's cousin who raised her as his own daughter) says to Esther, "For if you keep silent at this time, relief and deliverance will rise for the Jews from another place, but you and your father's house will perish. And who knows whether you have not come to the kingdom for such a time as this?" This verse speaks volumes to me. Think of that last sentence like this: "Perhaps you were born for a time such as this." Think about that. Perhaps you were born for this moment, this time, and this purpose. Perhaps God has put you exactly where you are just as He did Esther—to bring you a future that is more than you could imagine, to make a difference, to make a change, to help others come to know the Lord, to save someone. Esther was an orphaned slave girl who rose to become queen of the greatest empire of the time and to save an entire nation. She did not hold on to her past. She took risks and moved forward to a future and to fulfill her calling. When I start to dwell on the past, I think of Esther, and I remind myself that perhaps I was born for a time such as this. I focus my thoughts on all the incredible blessings God has given me, and I think how God has me exactly where He wants me at this moment. Maybe it is a moment of rest awaiting the next season of my life. Maybe it is in a storm, or maybe it is in a place of great joy. Wherever I am, I hold on to the fact that God has a plan for me, and it is a good plan. I just need to open my heart and listen, and He will guide me to walk in His mighty footsteps to the incredible future He has had planned for me since the beginning of time (Jeremiah 1:5).

Is the fear of the future holding you back from pursuing the dreams God has laid on your heart? Are you struggling with not trying to control what the future is and what it will bring? Do not worry; you are not alone. I still struggle in these areas, and I believe the fear of the future and trying to control it is what creates great anxiety for many. The following verses have helped me greatly in this area. They are well known verses and have helped me deal with facing the future and letting go of the anxiousness that comes from not knowing what lies ahead. I hope these verses help you in the same way.

> Do not be anxious about anything, but in everything by prayer and supplication with thanksgiving let your requests be made known to God. And the peace of God, which surpasses all understanding, will guard your hearts and your minds in Christ Jesus.
>
> Philippians 4:6–7 (ESV)

When I first learned these verses, I really did not understand them or how complex they were. Through study, I began to understand that if we come to God in prayer, humbly (supplication) giving Him thanks for all He has done and will do, then we can ask God for what our needs are. We should thank God in advance for answering our prayers because we trust God to answer all our prayers. We do not have to be anxious or worry because if we trust in the Lord, He will provide for *all* our needs—not just a few of them or some of them, but all of them. As we have discussed in earlier chapters, when you learn to give all your worries and cares to God, you will begin to experience the true peace of God. You will know an internal peace because instead of worrying about your problems and the future, you will be trusting God for all of them. That is how the peace of God guards our hearts and our minds in Christ Jesus. It is by removing the worry and anxiety from our hearts and minds and focusing on Jesus and His goodness that we find our minds guarded and protected from outside influences. These outside influences hold us in bondage as we keep fearing the future. We must release ourselves from these bondages of worry, fear, and control so God can do great works in us and for us.

"Trust in the Lord with all your heart, and do not lean on your own understanding. In all your ways acknowledge him, and he will make straight your paths" (Proverbs 3:5–6, ESV). I pray these verses almost every day. For someone like me who likes to control everything, these are perfect verses to memorize. They tell us that we must trust the Lord completely, and we cannot try to understand everything God is doing. If we try to understand, analyze, and control everything, we are not trusting God completely. We must know that there will be things in our lives we simply will not comprehend, and that is part of having faith in our Lord. In everything we do, we must acknowledge God or give Him thanks. Everything we have is because the Lord has so graciously allowed us to have it, so we should thank Him for everything. Finally, if we thank God in everything, He will make straight our paths. That means that if we obey God and trust Him, He will guide us straight forward to our future without all the curves and turns we make when we try to create our own path. What a wonderful promise this verse is! If we can learn to trust God, although there might be bumps along our path, He will guide us straight toward the future He so wants us to have.

When we look at our future with a positive attitude, filled with joy and hope instead of fear and disdain, we are walking in the path God wants us to walk. He wants us to look forward to the future and have dreams for what we want. He wants us to reach toward our goals. He wants to be part of everything we do and every decision we make. God is not just part of the equation; He is the equation! If we learn to let Him take control and always ask Him for guidance and listen to Him, He will lead us and show us what His great plans are for us and our future. God wants to help us more than anything because He loves us so very much. He wanted to help us so much that He gave His one and only Son to die on the cross for us. What more proof of His amazing love do we need than Jesus's death and crucifixion?

When we look at the future, we must always remember that tomorrow is never promised. We have no idea how many breaths God will grant us here on earth. If you have not accepted Jesus Christ as your Savior, do not put it off for one more day. While we might not know how many days, hours, or minutes we have left, we can rest in knowing that if we accept Jesus as our Savior, we can walk in eternity with God. That is one promise that has a 100 percent guarantee. If you would like to accept Jesus as your Savior today or if you are unsure if you are saved, please turn to the last page of this book where you will find a salvation prayer that you can say to ask Jesus Christ to come into your life as your Savior.

If you are already saved, wonderful! I hope you are excited about the future God has in store for you. Let's go back to the verse from the beginning of this chapter, Jeremiah 29:11 (NLT). "'For I know the plans I have for you,' says the Lord 'They are plans for good and not for disaster, to give you a future and a hope." God knows the plans He has for you. We must trust that His plans are good, and we must find hope in that. If you are like me and look back at your life twenty years ago, you probably thought your life was going to be very different than what it is. That is okay. It is more than okay. It is wonderful.

Yes, the road of life can be bumpy at times. There have probably been some potholes in the road. We have all made mistakes, but God has always been with us, and He has taken those mistakes and weaved them together to make the amazing story that is each of our lives. Every one of us has our own incredible story. God planned it that way. Psalm 139:14 (ESV) says, "For I am fearfully and wonderfully made. Wonderful are your works; my soul knows it very well." God made us in His image, and He has made each of us as an individual, incredible miracle. His works (us) are wonderful, and His works in our lives are amazing. So when you look toward the future, look at it with a zest for the life given to you by Jesus Christ. Know you were wonderfully made and that you are God's child. Open yourself up to what God wants you to do, and move forward. If you fail, that is okay. Get up, and try again. God will put you where He wants you, when He wants, and at just the right time—in His time. Be an Esther, and remember that you were created for a time such as this.

CHAPTER 15

Putting It All Together

When God our Savior revealed his kindness and love, he saved us, not because of the righteous things we had done, but because of his mercy. He washed away our sins, giving us a new birth and new life through the Holy Spirit. He generously poured out the Spirit upon us through Jesus Christ our Savior. Because of his grace he made us right in his sight and gave us confidence that we will inherit eternal life.

Titus 3:4–7 (NLT)

As we have journeyed through the past 14 chapters, we have discussed why we go through storms in our life and how to handle them. We have discussed letting doors close, learning to forgive, and moving on from our past. We have seen that miracles really do still happen and how important love is in each of our lives. We have spoken of surrendering our lives totally to God and letting God use us in His mighty way. As we have looked at all these topics, one theme has remained consistent: the incredible goodness of God and how He wants us to live a life full of joy, hope, and peace.

The above verses from the little-known book of Titus beautifully sum up the amazing goodness of God and the unbelievable gift we receive through Jesus Christ our Savior. Because of God's grace, His goodness, His kindness, His love, and His mercy, He chose to wash away our sins and give us a new life through the Holy Spirit. Because of Jesus, we were made right with God. We will never have to live separate from God again. We are His child, and we are totally forgiven and completely loved. We can live our life confidently knowing that if we have accepted Jesus Christ as our Savior, we will live an eternal life in heaven. It is my wish that when you finish the pages of this book, the words written by the Apostle Paul in Titus will be etched in your mind and heart. These words will speak to you in moments of incredible joy and insufferable sorrow. They will be with you in the light of day and the dark of night. You will cling tightly to them knowing how good our God is and how incredible the blessings and gifts are that He has given us through Jesus.

As you walk on your journey through life with God, remember that your journey is not just about the destination. It is about each step you take and how much you enjoy it along the way. Enjoy growing, changing, and becoming. When you feel like you still have so far to go, remember how far you have already come. Look at the incredible change God has allowed to happen in you, and be proud of the person you are becoming in Christ. When you stumble or fall during your journey, get back up, brush yourself off, and continue with God. When you grow tired and weary during your journey, take a seat, and rest in God. He will restore your soul. The longer you walk on your journey with God, the more your faith will grow. With each step you take, your trust in Him will become unshakable as you see the amazing blessings He gives you each day. You will move fluidly from season to season, glory to glory, with God as your rod and your staff, protecting you and comforting you (Psalm 23:4) each day of your life.

One thing we must never forget is that we do have an enemy, and he wants nothing more than for us to fail in our journey, our purpose, and our walk with God. Therefore, we must always remain focused and steadfast on our journey with the Lord. Hold tightly to the fact that "if God is for us, who can be against us?" (Romans 8:31, ESV). Our God is good, and He defeated the devil long ago on the cross. The devil is no challenger to our God who is our rock and our strong fortress. Nothing can come between us and our Father. As written in His Word:

> And I am convinced that nothing can ever separate us from God's love. Neither death nor life, neither angels nor demons, neither our fears for today nor our worries about tomorrow—not even the powers of hell can separate us from God's love. No power in the sky above or in the earth below—indeed, nothing in all creation will ever be able to separate us from the love of God that is revealed in Christ Jesus our Lord.
>
> Romans 8:38–39 (NLT)

Finally, remember that God is just not as good as we think He is. He is even better. He will always exceed our wildest expectations. All things are possible with God (Matthew 19:26). Nothing is too small for God. Come to Him with everything and for everything. God wants nothing more than to have a relationship with you. We are His family, His children. Relish your relationship with God, and love Him with complete abandonment as He does you. Accept the amazing forgiveness God has given you, and let go of all that is holding you back. Start your life anew today with Jesus by your side, knowing that no matter what you do or what you have done, He loves you the same as He did yesterday, as He does today, and as He will tomorrow. He loves you with an extraordinary love, a love that knows no bounds, a perfect love.

I leave you with one final set of verses. Paul's prayer in these verses is what I pray for each person who reads this book. May your life be filled with the strength, hope, peace, and joy that come from knowing God's amazing love.

> I pray that from his glorious, unlimited resources he will empower you with inner strength through his Spirit. Then Christ will make his home in your hearts as you trust in him. Your roots will grow down into God's love and keep you strong. And may you have the power to understand, as all God's people should, how wide, how long, how high, and how deep his love is. May you experience the love of Christ, though it is too great to understand fully. Then you will be made complete with all the fullness of life and power that comes from God.
>
> Ephesians 3:16–19 (NLT)

AFTERWORD

On March 23, 2020, I became unemployed for the first time in my life. Like more than 30 million Americans, the COVID-19 pandemic forced me out of work with a mandated shutdown in my state. I had to close the doors to my dance business for the foreseeable future. I had no idea what I would do, how I would pay my bills, or if my industry would survive a pandemic. In the beginning of the shutdown, I was like everyone else. I watched the news all the time. I saw the terrible loss of life around the world and the intangible suffering. The fear of the virus was very real. The fear of what lay ahead for me and my business crept into my mind, leaving me in tears many evenings. I felt helpless, so I did the only thing I could do. I prayed. I got down on my knees and prayed to my Father for help and guidance through these uncharted waters that not only I but the entire world was facing.

Then, as so often happens in our walk with the Lord, something incredible took place. God let me realize that this time of quarantine, which I felt was an insurmountable hurdle to jump over, was a gift—a blessing. It was a time for rejuvenation, introspection, and reflection. It was a time for growth in a way I would never have been able to experience if my everyday life had not been put on pause.

My eyes suddenly cleared from the blurry-eyed state of exhaustion I normally walked in, and I was able to see the small miracles Jesus was performing in my life every day. I took walks and enjoyed the incredible beauty of the creation God had surrounded me with in the town I live in. I smelled flowers, took in deep breaths of fresh air, and let the warm spring sun shine down on my face. I took car rides to nowhere, and I biked on trails I did not even know existed. I listened to sermons, read devotionals, studied the Bible, journaled, and prayed. I not only prayed, I also talked to God—a lot. My days were filled with an ongoing conversation with Him. I asked Him what He wanted me to learn during this time, what He wanted me to change in my life, and how He wanted me to grow.

As I spent more time focusing on God and our relationship, I began to gain an even deeper understanding that Jesus was what I needed more than anything in this world. I took a long, hard look at my life and knew that changes needed to be made. If I wanted to commit myself fully to the Lord, I would need to stop jam packing it full every moment with outside activities and distractions, and I would need to slow down. I would need to reassess what the priorities in my life were. I needed to stop living life running so hard and so fast that everything was passing by me in a blur. If I wanted to be able to hear from God, I would need to make time to quiet myself and my life so He could speak to me without cluttered thoughts jamming the airwaves of my mind.

During a time that by the world's standards should have been a deep, dark experience, a great light started to shine inside of me. I felt a joy and peace that I had never experienced before. I was starting to feel the true peace of the Lord.

I began to realize that I was not just changing; I was becoming. I was finally starting to become who God had intended me to be all along, not the person for so many years I had tried to become on my own. God did exactly what was in his Word (as He always does). "He lets me rest in green meadows; he leads me beside a peaceful streams. He renews my strength. He guides me along the right paths, bringing honor to his name" (Psalm 23:2–3, NLT). God literally gave me, along with millions around the world, a time to rest, rejuvenate, and take notice of what was important in my life and what was not. It was my choice if I took heed of what had happened and made the necessary changes or if I wandered in the desert around the same mountain for 40 years like the Israelites. I decided it was time for me to get out of the desert. Amid all the chaos in the world, I saw God working in my life and helping things fall into place. Once again, I am reminded how incredible and amazing our Father is. I am amazed how He always keeps His promises, and in Him we can always find hope and rest knowing that "despite all these things, overwhelming victory is ours through Christ, who loved us" (Romans 8:37, NLT).

SALVATION PRAYER

If you are ready to open your life to the Lord and accept Jesus Christ as your one and only true Savior, say the following prayer (out loud if you can).

> Dear Lord Jesus, I know I have lived a life of sin, and I ask for Your forgiveness. I believe You were crucified and died for my sins and rose from the dead. I no longer want to live a life separate from You. I ask You, Jesus, to please come into my life. I open my heart to You, and I accept You as my Lord and Savior. In Jesus's name, Amen!

You are now a new creation! And we are now both members of the same family of our Lord Jesus Christ.

CPSIA information can be obtained
at www.ICGtesting.com
Printed in the USA
BVHW040933240421
605735BV00005B/842